D0275263

THE GOOD TIMES

Also by James Kelman

An old pub near the Angel, and other stories
Three Glasgow Writers (with Tom Leonard and Alex Hamilton)
Short Tales from the Nightshift
Not not while the giro, and other stories
The Busconductor Hines
Lean Tales (with Agnes Owens and Alasdair Gray)
A Chancer
Greyhound for Breakfast
A Disaffection
Hardie and Baird & Other Plays
The Burn
Some Recent Attacks: Essays Cultural and Political
How late it was, how late

THE
GOOD
TIMES

JAMES
KELMAN

Secker & Warburg
LONDON

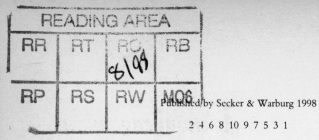

READING AREA

RR	RT	RO	RB
		8\98	
RP	RS	RW	MO6

Published by Secker & Warburg 1998

2 4 6 8 10 9 7 5 3 1

Copyright © James Kelman 1998

James Kelman has asserted his right under the Copyright, Designs
and Patents Act 1988 to be identified as the author of this work.

This book is sold subject to the condition that it shall not
by way of trade or otherwise, be lent, resold, hired out,
or otherwise circulated without the publisher's prior
consent in any form or binding or cover other than that
in which it is published and without a similar condition
including this condition being imposed on the
subsequent purchaser.

First published in Great Britain in 1998 by
Secker & Warburg
Random House, 20 Vauxhall Bridge Road,
London SW1V 2SA

Random House Australia (Pty) Limited
20 Alfred Street, Milsons Point, Sydney,
New South Wales 2061, Australia

Random House New Zealand Limited
18 Poland Road, Glenfield,
Auckland 10, New Zealand

Random House South Africa (Pty) Limited
Endulini, 5A Jubilee Road,
Parktown 2193, South Africa

Random House UK Limited Reg. No. 954009

A CIP catalogue record for this book
is available from the British Library

ISBN 0 436 41215 2

Papers used by Random House UK Limited are natural,
recyclable products made from wood grown in sustainable forests.
The manufacturing processes conform to the environmental
regulations of the country of origin.

Typeset by Palimpsest Book Production Limited,
Polmont, Stirlingshire
Printed and bound in Great Britain by
Mackays of Chatham PLC

Acknowledgements

Stories have appeared in the following publications: *A Fistful of Pens* (Derry, Northern Ireland); *Billy Liar* (Newcastle, England); *Ahead of its Time* (London, England); *Australian Short Stories* (Victoria, Australia); *Scottish Arts Foundation* (San Francisco, USA); *Paisley Writers Anthology* (Paisley, Scotland). A version of the story 'Comic Cuts' is a radio play entitled *The Art of the Big Bass Drum* which was broadcast on BBC Radio 3.

for
Marie
and
Laura and Emma

contents

Joe laughed
1

Gardens go on forever
10

pulped sandwiches
27

My eldest
47

It happened to me once
51

The Norwest Reaches
56

I was asking a question too
62

Yeh, these stages
69

Oh my darling
72

Every fucking time
90

Then later
125

Comic Cuts
128

Some thoughts that morning
180

The wey it can turn
188
sustenance sustenance
201
The Comfort
204
Into the Rhythm
216
Strength
225
Constellation
232
The Good Times
243

Joe laughed

It was nearly all derelict buildings down at the docks, most of them shells but some boarded up. Near the main road a couple of workshops and wee garages were open for business. Just behind them was a big scrapyard with cars piled high above the top of the walls. Security guys were supposed to be about the place and there was barbed wire but ye could still get in, the wall was bricks and there was bits where ye could fit in yer fingers. Once ye walked round the far side there was a great big patch of wasteground led clear down to the river. The surface was flat and we were using it for football but there was concrete patches so ye had to avoid tackling too heavy else ye were gony damage yer knees bad, then if ye landed on ragged metal or boulders, broken glass; even just if the concrete was rutted. Sliding in was out the question; naybody did it unless it was a mistake or they lost the head. One time Tugsy had to go to Casualty, a couple of us went with him, his knee was ripped open and his jeans were stuck with the blood. The nurse cut a big patch out and eftir they fixed him up that was that and he just had to go hame, this big hole with the bandage showing through, and the leg of his jeans hinging down. He had to get jags in the side of his knee and they used a scrubbing brush on it, they put a red ointment stuff on first then they scrubbed it. Tugsy said he didnay know what was ointment and what was blood. That was how they put the ointment on, so ye couldnay tell which was which. He watched them doing it. He didnay feel a thing cause they had froze the knee; one

1

of the jags was for tetanus. So although the place was good there were drawbacks.

Then too the ball made wild bounces on the concrete. That and the force of the wind. Ye wouldnay have played there during the winter. When somebody done a crazy kick the wind caught it and it flew for ages. It was a wonder it didnay go stoating right into the water. And cause there was nay give in the ground ye couldnay get yer foot under the ball right and yer heel jarred, ye had to use yer toes. But it still suited the ball-player, ye controlled it first time just, and kept it low.

We didnay know how long it would last, we expected a squadcar to pull up any day and tell us tae get to fuck. Maybe they would maybe they wouldnay. Maybe they wouldnay bother, that was what some of the guys thought. At first we used to keep an eye open but then eftir that we didnay, we just forgot, I did anyway. The games were good. It was different age-groups and it was serious, people played serious. Even if the score went wild, it just meant we shifted the sides. This game was like that and me, Joe and Perce went for a walk. It was a spell when the clouds were away and the sun was beating down. A couple of the aulder guys shouted at us but we just carried on walking. It was into September but ye felt if ye could have trusted the water ye would have been diving in and swimming. There was nay chance of that but it was all clogged up with shite, oil and liquid stuff skimming the surface. It was a right heavy smell. When ye looked down ye could see bedsteads and motor cars and auld fucking everything. I had a fag and we smoked it. We were seeing how far we could pitch boulders, watching the plunge. It seemed like the bigger the boulders the less disturbance they caused the water except the sound was bigger and deeper. Perce was doing the usual show-off, his boulders were heavier and he tossed them further. I couldnay have cared less, it was daft. Forget to let go, I said but quiet, so he wouldnay hear me. Joe was laughing and Perce looked back, wondering what it was about. He didnay have to get telt but, he knew it was me. There was aye a bit of needle between the two of us. I annoyed him he annoyed me, that was the way it went. Joe didnay care. I didnay either. I was the best player out the young team, I always got picked first. Sometimes I got picked afore a couple of the aulder yins. A pitch like this suited me, the way I played the game. It didnay suit Perce, he was an out-and-out defender, never happy unless he was kicking fuck out somebody, especially if it was me, but he couldnay get fucking near me. They were gony change the teams for the second half cause it was a big score. I was hoping to be against Perce, I would run rings round him, he wouldnay get touching the ball, it would be through his legs and fucking everywhere, he had fucking nay chance, I was looking forward to it; I felt it in my belly, I was gony fucking do him. We headed back.

The rest of the guys were sitting about, a few were playing cards. It would be a while afore the restart so we kept walking, ower the auld factory buildings. There was one we had seen the last time and wanted to check out. It had a window on the first floor with its glass out. I went up the rone-pipe and it was easy, a lot of joints and places for yer feet. In through the window, it was dark and musty. Parts of the ceiling hung down with white powdery sheets and stuff sticking out. A lot of bricks and cardboard and rusty auld nails. It was obvious the place had been gutted so there wasnay gony be nothing lying about. I shouted down to the other two but Perce said he was wanting to explore. I telt them it was gutted and how the Security was supposed to be there guarding it but Perce said sometimes they just stuck up the notices to con ye and Joe says just to try and find a door.

I found one when I went down the stairs. Again it was the same story as up above, if there had been anything worth taking it wasnay here now; long gone. There was a big bar across the door but it just lifted off and there was nay padlock, I opened it nay bother. Joe and Perce came in right away and when I shut it Perce battered me on the shoulder and ran off laughing. Joe ran with him, shouting round at me. I chased for a wee while then chucked it when they disappeared through another room. I waited for them to come back but they didnay, I just went up the first floor again. I found a corridor and went along and there was an open kind of iron staircase. It was great. Ye could see through it as ye climbed. It took ye up through the roof to the next floor and here was one great big room. It looked like somebody had swept it clean. There was nothing in it at all, no even rubbish. I heard the other two yelling on me from below but I didnay bother, I couldnay be arsed. I was annoyed at them as well, what they were doing was childish. I wanted to disappear from them never mind the other way about.

I went through another door and there was an ordinary side staircase. It led up to the top landing which was an attic with slanted ceilings and skylights. What a place! It had been swept clean tae except I saw a pile of rubbish stored at a wall. I checked it out. It was mainly dirt and broken glass, the usual bits of wood and cardboard, rusty nails. There was a funny smell but, like shite. I found auld newspapers in a corner, yellow on the top but white inside. Football reports frae years ago. It was funny seeing the photies of the players. Robbie McManus was there and he had a full head of hair, he looked good. I tore the page out and put it in my pocket. I heard somebody whistle loud and it left an echo, it wasnay Joe.

4

At the far end of the space was another door and it opened into a wee room with a desk and a chair lying on its side. Three legs and a stump was all it had. I stood it up and gave it a push and it toppled. I done it again. Then I saw a safe. I couldnay believe it; it was just sitting there. The door was open; just and no more. It was so thick ye had to really pull it. I knew there was gony be nothing in it but I searched high and low, feeling about at the corners and looking for nooks and crannies. I didnay expect nothing anyway. Somebody aye got there afore ye.

When I slammed the door shut it clunked home but then creaked open and went to where it had been afore, its hinges werenay working right. I pushed and hauled at the desk, getting it close to the wall, in beneath the window, so as I could climb up. I went onto my tiptoes to see out but the window was high and I couldnay see the pitch. I wondered where the other two had got. Maybe they were still on the ground floor. But naw, surely they would have went exploring. If so they would have come up here. Unless they hadnay bothered. It was a pain in the neck. Just the way they done it, the way they ran off like that, it was annoying. I couldnay hear any noises so I dont think the game had restarted, but maybe it had.

The way the roof angled the view was a way ower and I couldnay see out properly at all, no unless I could stretch up higher. Maybe the game had restarted. Uch aye, it would have. Who cares, cause I didnay. Except it was annoying. I was annoyed at Joe as well. A joke's a joke but this was beyond the score. Perce was a fucking idiot so he was, a bampot, I couldnay care less about him. It was just how Joe had went with him, that was what annoyed me. It really did. A joke's a joke. I just thought fuck him, fuck the two of them. I couldnay care less. No even about the football, if I didnay

5

finish the game. I wasnay even sure if I was ever gony play ever again. I'm talking about ever, for the rest of my life. I felt I wouldnay, I felt I didnay want to. I felt like I had kicked my last ball. And I was fucking glad. I was never gony fucking kick another fucking ball again in my whole fucking life and I was fucking glad, that was that, I had fucking finished with it, fucking football, I was finished. I loved football tae, I loved it. That was the amazing thing. There was nothing I loved more. There was nothing else except it. Kicking a ball about, it was the only thing. I could imagine what they would all say. My auld man. He would be shocked. They would all be shocked. I couldnay care fucking less. The game on Saturday. I didnay even know who we were playing, I couldnay even remember, and it didnay fucking matter cause that was me I was finished. If the auld man wanted to go and watch it then that was good go ahead but he was gon alone cause I wasnay playing, that was one thing.

I was on my tiptoes trying the window, it was heavy and stiff and wouldnay budge. I got down off the desk and lifted the chair onto it and got it on its side against the wall, then got back up and tested it for standing; it was alright, I could use it nay bother. My head was up past the sill and I could get most of my force for pushing. I heaved and got it open, but then it stuck halfway, less, it jammed. But I could hear a couple of the boys shouting. It sounded far away, like the pitch was right away ower the other side of the docks. I dived up my arms through the gap, then my head and shoulders. I got my elbows wedged ower the sill to take my weight. I waited, getting my breath. The roof was about five feet below. I got a shiver, that bit of dizziness ye get, my head gon that roomy way, I had to shut my eyes a wee minute.

If I dreeped down onto the roof it would be too hard getting back up again because of the slope. I would have

6

to be dead careful even doing the dreeping because of it, if I staggered one wee bit I would be down the slope and right off the edge. No unless I could get at the gutter maybe get my foot wedged in. But it would be hopeless, I would be coming down the slope too fast. It would be one go, that was all I would get. And if I didnay get it that was that.

I pulled myself right up now taking my weight on my arms. Then I let my feet touch back down. I wasnay wanting to go yet, no all the way, no till I knew how to get back. I thought I would make it but, once I got out on the ledge. I pulled myself back up again to look. Aye, I thought I could dreep down slow, get my toes touching on the slates, just touching, getting my balance.

I wasnay scared. I liked roofs and was used to them but they were tricky and ye couldnay trust auld yins cause of the slates; and they moved too much, ye had to take it one step at a time, ye had to go slow. I wasnay even sure I would find the rone-pipe. There was a lot of big weeds growing out the gutter. I saw one like a tree coming out a chimney. So it would be hard finding it. Except there had to be one somewhere cause it wasnay one of these roofs where there are bits go up and down and round corners, it was just a plain yin. Sometimes ye could look for birds and see where they were nesting and it meant the rone might be near. But even if I did find it, some gutters went out too far. That was what I was worried about, climbing ower, if there was nay grips. The best thing would be dreeping down frae the window but then gon up the way instead of down. Once I was at the top of the roof I would be able to see everything.

My arms were getting sore under the armpits. I got down off the chair then off the desk and I sat down on the floor with my back to the wall. The thing is naybody could climb higher than me. Any roof at all and I would climb it, ye had to be light and strong and able to pull yerself right up, and that was me, I could climb a rope just using my hands and arms, nay bother, and going up a rone was easy, I could wedge my toes in on nothing, just the pipe and the wall; I could turn and wave down to people, it didnay worry me; sometimes I went dizzy but I aye just waited it out, I closed my eyes or else stared into the stone, then I got my bearings. The place I stayed I was known for it. If any of the women forgot their keys I was the boy they called on, I could fly up the wall and in the veranda. I done it for nothing. If they gave me money sometimes I didnay even take it. Even if they didnay offer it, I wouldnay have took it if they had. My maw didnay like me doing it but sometimes I done it for her too and my da kidded on he didnay know. It was funny when I saw the women looking up at me, their hands up at their mouth, if I was gony make it; but it was nothing, I wondered how come they were worried; I knew how far it was frae joint to joint. I didnay even have to look up. Sometimes I climbed up past the veranda ledge just because well it didnay matter. And then once I was inside their hoose I would gie them a wave. But it wasnay always easy because sometimes they had locked the veranda door and I had to jump back onto the ledge and get across from there to the sill on the bathroom window, and that was tricky cause it was a stretch, there was nay grip except the side bricks there, all ye could do was fix yer hand tight and edge out using yer knees, keeping yer hand gripped and then pulling yerself across; from there but I liked swinging out and crouching, my feet on the sill and my hands gripping the inside frame on the wee top window, afore getting my hand through and down to the handle at the side window. I would stay there perched, letting one of my legs dangle ower the edge, seeing them looking up frae below. Then I pulled the window open and in I went and the woman would come up and I would open the front door for her and her kids and that was that, that was how I done it, it was easy, I was used to it, I didnay care, that was how they called for me, well they could call for me all their life, that was how long they could call, that was from now on, cause I was finished with it; I wasnay sure what I was gony do, no from now on, I maybe no even do nothing, it would just depend.

Gardens go on forever

Quarter of an hour later the horn beeped and I tugged on the shoes fast, slipped the book into my inside jacket pocket and rushed out, slamming shut the door, probably wakening the entire house. My new abode tae, maybe they would chuck me out for noisy conduct. Downstairs two and three steps at a jump, out and across the street where the transit van was jittering and shuddering. The driver kicked off even before I got in properly. Christ sake, I shouted, one leg trailing outside. But he wouldnay have heard me. He was one of the tensest guys I knew and driving this heap of shite made him worse. It was like he had to drive fast as fuck in case the engine packed in, so he could get to the destination before it happened.

The engine was always packing in. There was some undia-gnosed trouble with the fuel-pump but the boss said every time he tried a garage they couldnay find the problem, so he was paying dough for nothing; the usual rubbish, any fucking excuse, he was a total cheapskate. Then the back door itself, last man in had to hold the fucking thing shut else it flew open round corners. Even a bit of string might have done the job but no doubt there was a good business reason how come it didnay happen. I wasnay gony say a word, that was one thing I was learning, no to open my mouth. But I mumped and grumped and looked about. To no avail. The three guys in the back of the van were locked into last night's dreams and nightmares although one of them had his eyes open – this was Adam, a new guy, like myself, still finding it a mind-blowing exercise, this getting out of bed at the same time every morning. It was like pre-dawn or something, the world a damp and fresh place to be, schoolkids and all kinds of extraordinary stuff. According to rumour once we got to the end of the season it would still be dark when we went to work. A likely story. This was bad enough, the idea people were sleeping snug in bed for another two or three hours. Life was unfair. Especially if it was a male and he was tucked up with a beautiful woman. Some males do get tucked up with beautiful women. One of these days I would become one of them. Nothing was more certain than that. If certainty existed then so did she.

Ho hum. If one could choose to work or not work one would choose the option that allowed a lifestyle that made one a normal fellow. Routines like this could scarcely be normal, I refused to believe it. Any hero would have banged on the partition separating us from the driving cabin, told the driver to stop and then, after a parting sally to the rest of the squad, that would be that, away to fuck, fashioning a more dignified mode of existence. I wanted the stars!

That was the right way. Ambition. Why should everything be defined by work that returned financial profit? Why not work that was great in itself and who cares three fucking hoots about monetary returns! I wanted to question whether such returns were indeed a profit. A profit to the individual person. I couldnt believe it wouldnt not be the case. I could fall for a lot of stuff but not that. It was just a mode of mind-control. The snoring from one of the guys interrupted my thinking; Sidney McGowan, my sidekick and partner, he of the sick imagination, unacknowledged alcoholic. Lazy bastard into the bargain. Unless it was a result of the booze. Maybe it was genuine, part of the condition. Next to him was old Jake, he was snoozing as well.

Naw but I have to confess I liked Sidney. Just as well. It

11

must be a nightmare working beside somebody ye hate. I couldnay imagine that. Of course he had his bad points, a lot of bad points. He skived off half the time. Mind you that wasnay a problem because I was beginning to quite like the job's physicality factor. I hadnay at first, it took a bit of getting used to. But now! Well . . . maybe I had found my metier, my life's thingwi, a reason to believe and all that shite, who knows. Just if I could have defined my own terms and conditions! Fucking hell! Because yes, I liked this physicality factor, it was having the opposite of a detrimental effect on my body. I looked in the mirror at night and sometimes did the muscle-flexing act with the upper arms. It was great as long as I avoided seeing myself too close, otherwise I could burst out with a weird sort of laugh, it wasnay really a laugh, it was more like a yowl, whatever that is. Nothing to do with an anguished soul. Nevertheless, I was quite happy when Sidney skived off to find a likely hidey-hole, it was like gon to an outdoor gymnasium and getting two workouts for the price of one. He had quite good patter as well – daft, it suited me. When I asked how come he was called Sidney he telt me his old man was a merchant sailor. That was that. I went to the pub and got drunk with him a few times. He could get steamboats just with the smell of the first pint. Then again he could go for hours, I would be a dribbling wreck and he would still be sitting there, checking out whether or not he could with impunity steal my unfinished lager. That was the kind of bastard he was. He also had the habit of walking out on me! He would tell me he was gon for a slash then disappear. Two hours later I would remember he hadnay come back and still being an innocent I would have to go and check out the cludgie in case he had fallen asleep. I refused to believe a sane person could walk out on my company. So that was Sidney, an insane bastard. And old Jake sitting next to him, I didnay

trust his snoozing, not at all, why the hell should I? These
ancient bastards, because they're set for the high jump we're
supposed to treat them with tender caution.

So that was the three of them, my workmates. Plus
the driver. Plus the boss. Then too ye got the customers,
these amazing fuckers whose gardens we transformed from
rainforest jungles into pretty green patches. I took the book
out my pocket and opened a page at random:

> However, in typical finite experience the dimensions of
> temporality lack such wholeness and are usually in a state
> of imbalance. One or other of the three dimensions of
> temporality has come to have undue predominance.

It was oh so easy to translate this to my immediate surroundings. Where did it all take you though?

> There is a quest for a wholeness of experience or an
> immediacy of fruition that would gather up in itself past,
> present and future.

It was incredible how you could make something of the
words; an uncanniness about it as well: these coincidences,
where random book-openings make the most pertinent sense
in terms of where and how you happen to be in the world,
especially when it is somebody else's book which when it
happens is both a wonder and a beauty. I debated for a split
second whether to wake up Sidney and read it to him. Or
else there was Adam, gazing into the void. Being the new
guy he didnay speak very much. Maybe he didnay get the
chance, or else he was just quiet by nature. Or else he had
fuck all to say. Maybe his head was the void, or maybe he

13

was sitting there racking his brains for something pertinent to talk about and by the time he found it us three were off on a different topic.

Now the book shut, the driver having braked quite suddenly. That was the page lost. It didnay matter. Past, present and future. Working in a job like this a body understood these finer details. Twenty minutes later I would be holding a pair of garden shears merciful heavens. Never mind. Better than the spade or pitchfork, the pitchfork being the better of these two efforts but either way I wound up with a bruised instep. My shoes were soft. They werenay really shoes at all. It was a pair of Docs I needed, I was saving for them. How could I grumble but with a job, any job, just being able not to have to go to that fucking government fucking place, it did the old brain a power of good. Not the heart. Which rightly suggested that the wage I drew was scarce compensation for lost freedoms. Lost freedoms cannot be regained. Not the ones I'm talking about. One day last week for instance I could have been off climbing mountains or sailing the high seas. In fact I should have been off climbing mountains or sailing the high seas. It was my own fault I hadnay. I allowed a dictatorial state to determine my existence. What can one do! That was the kind of shit I asked myself. What can one not do? Now there's the real way of talking about one's life, authentic stuff.

Hoy Mikey boy what's that ye're reading? Jake had returned to consciousness. He didnay snore as much as Sidney but I think his sleep was deeper, if sleep it was. He was closer to death, probably that was it. The closer it approached the more ye prepared for it. Sometimes I wondered about old guys, how they went on. At the same time Jake had an inquisitive mind. I showed him the title. What's it about? he said.

Adam was interested as well. Here, I said, I'll read yez a bit, get some higher thoughts into yer dreich existences. I flicked to a page at random and landed at precisely the same spot as before: However, I said, in typical finite experience the dimensions of temporality lack such wholeness and are usually in a state of imbalance. One or other of the three dimensions of temporality has come to have undue predominance. That's plenty. I closed the book.

Who wrote it? said Jake.

I showed him the title-page.

German? he said.

I showed him the page with the author information.

You read this stuff a lot dont ye?

Well no all the time, sometimes I go to the cludgie. Having said that, I usually take it with me. But there's nay law against reading books in cludgies.

There is if folk are waiting to get in.

If I could read books while I was digging a trench then I'd fucking do it. I've been trying to invent something that would haud it in front of my nose.

Reading while ye work?

Yeh.

What about one of these mouthorgan-things that Bob Dylan has? take aff the mouthorgan and fasten on a book.

That's a great idea.

Or else ye could use that carrot-contraption they stick in front of donkeys.

Ho hum.

It's the same thing Mikey boy I'm no being cheeky.

Ah well, aye, ye might have something there. I'll do some architectural drawings the night when I get hame. I'm doing fuck all anyway, it's no as if I've got a beautiful woman waiting for me, somebody that'll make my tea and then lead me to a four-poster bed. Wait and I'll read ye this bit: There is a quest for a wholeness of experience or an immediacy of fruition that would gather up in itself past, present and future.

Sounds to me like ye're talking about getting yer hole.

Exactly, that's how I read ye.

Course ye never think of Germans and sex, more like fitba.

Well, they've some rare players.

They've aye had rare players, I mean how many times have they won the World Cup now?

Three.

Ye sure it's no four?

There was that time England fucked them at Wembley with the hometown decision, the '66 game.

Aw aye, said Jake, I mind that yin mysel – Alf Ramsey, he fucking hated us. Cause we aye beat them. Alf Ramsey, he spoke like the fucking Queen; yous'll no mind.

We aye beat the English? I said.

Aye back then we did, I'm talking about the days we used to play them. Funny thing but we were a crabbit bunch of bastards at the same time. Nowadays every cunt gubs us and we're fucking cheery about it. Maybe if we stopped being so fucking cheery we'd start winning again. The tartan army and aw that crap, we used to be the worst hooligans of the fucking lot. See this stuff about good-natured fans? it's a load of shite. I mind the five one game at Wembley, rivers of pish running down the stairs. Every cunt just cocked the leg and said Fuck it. Ye want to have seen it but they were rampaging. They tore up that fountain at Trafalgar Square, fucking pawned it I think – that's what I'd have done, fucking halfwits, nay point getting huckled for fuck all know what I mean, if ye're no earning a few quid?

Where are we? said Adam.

The Stockiemuir, I said, judging by the bumps and curves.

Fucking Stockiemuir my arse, said Jake, that's the wheels falling off. Away back to yer book and gie us peace.

Listen to fucking Santa Claus, I said.

Santa Claus! where does he get them!

Sidney's eyes were open, now he closed them, just in time, the eyeballs looked like they were about to fall out. Later me and him got dumped at our field of a garden. He got out first. As soon as my feet touched the ground the driver shot off, carrying my book with him. I shouted and waved but there was nay stopping the bastard. Sidney was standing by the gate, his body going through a heavy shivering stage.

The hedges were gigantic as fuck and down at the street-end were a lot of trees, the branches hanging out onto the pavement. Dont say we've got to cut all that? I said.

Sidney shook his head, he brought the irn bru out his bag, swigged a mouthful, smacked his lips and had another go, then he put the bottle away.

Thanks.

What's up? he said.

Fuck all.

Ye in a bad mood cause they've took yer book?

Naw I'm no in a bad mood cause they've took my book. Nay fucking time to read anywey, no with you as a mate.

You dont know when ye're well aff.

True.

When I followed him inside the gate the size of the place took my breath away. It's like a fucking national park! This guy must be a millionaire.

He's a multi-millionaire ken he's a dental surgeon. He's got private practices all ower the place.

Ye kidding?

Naw.

17

Has he got a swimming pool out the back? cause if he has I'm gon for a dip.

This kind of statement was of a form Sidney ignored at his leisure. He led the way round the back of the house to where the gardening utensils were stored in a poky wee shed athwart a seventeen-car garage. I didnay know dental surgeons made this kind of money, I said, so they're wealthy fuckers eh!

They can be, aye, they work hard for their dough but.

I didnay pursue the point. Sidney had a habit of pulling these right-wing comments out of nowhere. When he reached the door into the shed he stopped and lifted his leg: a rupture of a fart. It was an obscenity the way he done it.

It's human nature, he said.

No to lift yer leg it isnay, that's an emphasis. Ye're emphasising the fart.

I'm no emphasising the fart it's just the wey it comes.

Ye could've at least went round the back of the hut Sidney christ almighty it isnay even windy. Naw nay kidding.

He shook his head. I'm putting on the tea, d'ye want some?

Ye making a fire?

If I have to.

You're a fucking danger.

I'm a fire-expert son, he said, walking off towards the garden-shed.

Well I'm gony scab in, I shouted, I want to get my muscles in trim; there's a long life ahead and I'm gony be prepared.

Sidney gave me a vee sign ower the shoodir. I walked after him. Heh maybe he's prepared for ye, I said, maybe he's got a video camera hiked up a tree. That's what they do these multi-millionaires, they spy on the home-helps, I'm talking about Mister Bones the tooth doctor.

Mister Bones the tooth doctor! Mikey boy ye're a case

18

– a fucking head-case. The shears are in the shed by the way.

Jesus mary and joseph my bollocks, I hope they're blunt.

Dont start with that gruesome patter.

Me? It's you, it's you started it; all these nightmare tales frae yer gardening past.

Deep down ye're scared to get married.

Rubbish.

I pity the poor lassie whoever she is.

Pity her, pity her . . . !

I'm away to fill the kettle.

Whereabouts?

Somewhere.

Right.

And off went he, leaving me to the garden-shed which was falling to fucking bits as per fucking usual. According to these silly bastards on television the insides of said structures have a beauty all their own. The pundits talk about them like they're Santa's Grotto. A great and wide-ranging assortment of damp odours etcetera, the beauties of the natural world. Semi-buddhist crap. If I spent too long inside them it done my nut; panic, dread and the gloomiest angst imaginable. This had nothing to do with creepy crawlies of which I'm quite fond, speaking as a cityboy born and bred thank fuck, and thank fuck again. Imagine having to wear corduroy trousers all the time.

I got the shears and worked solid for nearly two hours, lost in a world of daydreams. But emotionally charged stuff. I went through an entire gamut. From annoyance at multi-millionaire dental surgeons and niggardly bosses through horrific excruciating nightmares, mounting excitement, the sensation of eureka, sexual arousement, fantasy deaths in the family, revolutionary practices towards laying the foundation

19

to a genuine workers' republic right here in good old bonny Scotland, then the obvious, my early cessation – not just the funeral (at which my unknown beautiful wife would weep fulsome tears at my early demise, cut off at my prime) but the wake and celebratory post-demise musings.

Mind you, says Jake, he was a good boy deep down. I'll drink to that, says Sidney.

But at the end of it all I was left with Rob Weston the moviestar as an underrated actor. What a let down. At the same time I thought yeh, Rob Weston, christ, he is a fine actor, just waiting for the correct parts to come along. If I was his agent I would know how to handle him properly. I'd make a point of it; it would be good for morale, not only for him and me but for the other actors in the stable. It would make them feel less stressed-out, now that the only work they get is comic walk-ons for tomato sauce and beer adverts. What's the point, even if ye do make a million bucks, there's more to life than profit and loss. And what do we mean by loss anyway? If it comes to that, what do we mean by a million bucks? Do they even call them bucks nowadays, in the good old U.S. of A.! Maybe it's just televisual shite, maybe it's the old greenbacks, a million greenbacks.

These kind of thoughts crowd out my skull when I'm working. I'm a fucking crackpot. I ordered myself to stop it at once, quit the nonsense, shut up shut up shut fucking up, but there was nay use covering my ears although this is what I caught myself about to do. I knocked off to find Sidney, and found a tap plumbed in at the outside wall of the garage and had a good-going wash, my first of the day. This new place I was living in wasnt too good on the cleanliness front, the bathroom was a bit of a fucking nightmare to be honest. Once I found out the situation with the other tenants I would consider giving it a tidy – that's if they were working as a team. But no if they were

20

lazy bastards, I wasnay gony be any sort of unpaid do-gooding stupit fucking skivvy.

Sidney had vanished again. His wife was an angel or a saint. Maybe she was a martyr. My mother was a martyr. That was how I left home at the age of eighteen. Now here I was, a hand to mouth existence and damn fucking sick of it, damn fucking sick of it.

There was nay shops for miles. Sidney had the tea things set out in a snug clearing enclosed by sweet-smelling bilberry trees (only joking); two mugs for two mugs and a pair of kit-kat biscuits which he always referred to as a meal in itself. A meal in itself, he said.

He took on the role of provider, a tacit apology for the fact he done fuck all work. But sometimes I got the feeling he was a trifle uneasy at my devil-may-care tactics. He might have been a right-wing bastard but the moral imperative was not lost on him. At least the sun isnay shining, he said, mind you it's no so cold as it was. He sat down, sighing, unwrapping the silver paper, gazing fondly at the chocolate biscuit, then set to with the gihnashers.

Heh, what about that Rob Weston the actor? I said.

What?

Rob Weston, he's been in tons of movies, comedy things. What I'm talking about is his overall acting ability. As far as I'm concerned he's underrated. A guy in my digs had a video out last night and before I knew where I was I was watching it with him. A comedy; but the part he was playing called for some of the real stuff. I didnay expect to like it in the first place so I quite enjoyed it for that reason alone. Comedies can be a let down. Usually they're no funny. I didnay think this one was gony be funny either.

So what did ye get it out for?

It wasnay me that got it out it was another guy. What

I'm saying but the part Rob Weston had, it was real out-of-character. It showed what he could do if they gave him a chance, the hollywood moguls.

Mmm. Sidney frowned. If it's the guy I'm thinking about I aye found him a bit stupit looking, like he's trying to be something he isnay ken as if he's just kidding on. I wouldnay take him seriously son, being honest.

That's exactly it but that's what I'm saying. I thought that tae; thought, past tense. Now I'm beginning to think if he got the right part he could do it, he really could. He's definitely got it in him. There's a lot of them could do it, if they got the right parts; but they dont, ye see them doing these walk-ons and ye think fuck they're real actors, they're trained at it, they could take the lead, they could do it. And they could do it, if somebody gave them the chance. They just dont get the chance. Ye're talking about the star-system, the way it's geared to big bucks, mega-bucks.

There's merr tae it than that.

I dont think so.

D'ye know any actors?

Aye.

Who?

A couple

What's their names?

Joe Rafferty and Bill Thomas, they drink in that local of mine. Naw sorry, I cannot tell a lie, I just made that up. I dont know what their names are. But they do drink in that local of mine.

What is their names?

I dont know.

Well how d'ye know they're actors?

Somebody telt me. They come in quite a lot. I think one of them's been on the stage a few times, it's no just adverts they do. What I'm saying but see if they got the chance, they could do a real job. But the bigwigs'll no gie them a chance, they'll no gamble. That's how the industry's falling apart, tales of woe everywhere, all these movies, they're all making a loss. Millions and millions of pounds, all down the tubes. That's what happens.

That's what what happens?

The money, it fucking disappears.

It doesnay fucking disappear son somebody's coining it. Somebody's got to be coining it. Ken what I mean, it doesnay go up in smoke.

Aye, right, I'm talking about that.

It doesnay vanish into thin air.

I know christ that's what I'm saying. When ye think about it, what does going-down-the-tubes actually mean? it actually doesnay have a meaning, it just disguises the fact some rip-off merchant's making a fucking fortune. Who but?

The banks.

Of course; aye, that's right. They'll no be happy till they're doing their own minting.

They're doing that already son.

Right, yeh.

Then as well as that ye've got the breweries, they're worth a fortune tae. In fact son these breweries have got more assets than the whole of fucking Africa and South America put the gether, so there is a revolution coming – never you mind yer politics and philosophy books.

It's no just them I read. I read other stuff. Africa and South America have got big assets anywey, it's just they're in the wrong hands.

Aye well obviously.

Everything's in the wrong hands.

Especially when they're having a pish.

See if I had money Sidney know where I'd put it? Public utilities, these things the public have got to have, if they dont they die. It's no the luxuries in life that make the money, it's the essential requisites. Put a tax on fresh air, that's what I would do if I was the government.

They done it already son that was the poll tax.

I'm no talking about that but, just fresh air; we could liquidise it then bottle it up, we could sell it, we could fucking sell it.

They sell it already, it's called water, liquid oxygen. The brewery scientists are finding a way to put a heid on it. See when they do we'll all go out and swally it doon ken two quid a pint, that's what they're gony charge us.

How dae you know?

Cause they telt me, I'm a brewery consultant, they've got me on their mailing list; whenever they try out a new product I'm the man they send for ken I've got my own dirty cloot.

Dirty cloot?

A special one reserved, I've got it reserved.

From this point on he lost me, I shut my ears. He criticised me for my patter but his was worse. When I first worked with him he came out with all these gruesome yarns from his gardening past; crazed shears and dangling bollocks, holly bushes and falling in nude head first. Sick stuff. I was worried and took it personal till he came out with one when we were going home in the van; with others in the company I knew it was alright. Jake gave me a wink and a nudge. Sidney's tales for young boys, he said, dont worry about it, it's all symbolic. Aye but symbolic of what? that was what I wanted to know. Virginity or the loss of manhood, what? I was twenty-four for fuck sake no a kid.

I got the shears and returned to work, needless to say I

was thinking about being dead. I couldnay stop it. It was Sidney's fault although usually I do think about it. But just now it was more real and that was what was his fault. It was away to a time about seventy years on. So it was true and there was no possibility of being alive, I definitely would be dead. If I wasnay I would be hitting a hundred. Who wants to be a hundred. Of course there is always exceptions, ye read about these parts of the world where auld guys go on and on forever. This story I read once where a traveller finds himself in a Himalayan-style environment and comes out the other side of a wooded mountain and meets up with these men tilling the soil and it turns out they're all ancient, there's some special thing about the air or else the plant-life and they just go on and on until they're about who knows, two hundred or something.

Sidney was shouting at me. I'm away to wash the cups, then I'm finding a quiet corner!

What happens if Mister Bones turns up?

He'll no.

Missis Bones?

I dont know about her.

What about Daughter Bones, maybe there's a Daughter Bones?

Maybe there is, said Sidney, I wouldnay know. He turned on the tap to wash out the mug, then he called: Tell ye one thing but, I'm no surprised you're a bachelor.

I'm no a bachelor, I've just no met the right woman.

Aye well ye never will, no the wey you're going.

Fuck off.

Dont say I didnay warn ye. Ye'll no face up to life and one of these days ye've got to. See that ancient auld tree round the back, the weeping willow, the one that's gigantic as fuck?

The one that's full of flies, bees, spiders, moths and butterflies, aye, so what?

It's no full of goblins son ken what I'm saying?

Okay dokey.

I watched to see him smile but he didnay, he just gave me a look and then went round the back of the shed. I battered on for a wee while then stopped, wiped off the sweat from my neck and then round under my chin, which for some reason is the place I seem to get it.

pulped sandwiches

I dont smell nothing, I told you that.

Ye sure?

I am sure. How many times!

Okay okay.

He didnay smell nothing but I did, it was there in my nostrils. I was sitting with the pack of sandwiches on my lap, I had a cigarette burning. He was reading that newspaper. He had his head bent so he was concentrating. He was putting that over. I couldnay talk to him. I tried, I couldnay. He got into them fucking moods. But it wasnay just that. Then too I was thinking things. My head was fucking full of it. It was him, he got talking then it was me. Then he shut up and I was left there. I wished I hadnay been talking, I wished I didnay have to talk ever again. That was how I felt, this job piece of shit, I couldnay fucking breathe. There wasnay any goddam fucking air. I felt it in my lungs, the fucking space, tightness; trying to draw a breath, no fucking breath to draw. This place. I wouldnay have spoke anyway except for him. I let him prattle on, I was away thinking about me and the missis, how by the time the holidays came the good weather would be done. What would we do then? We could still go and see the sea. No just from the hotel window cause we got out; hail, rain or shine, we always got out. She said she was dragging me down the coast if she had to but she didnay have to do no fucking dragging, she knew me well enough, I liked the sea as much as she did. Better, I liked it better. That salt and the air, that wind, and freshness and

27

fucking beautiful blowing at ye, ye felt it, closing yer eyes into it jesus.

Dan was looking at me now, looking sideways. He was wanting me in on a gamble. Friday. I wasnay in the mood. Never mind the dough it cost when did he ever win? He never won. Then he went about moaning and groaning. Dan, I said, when ye gony get some fucking wisdom into yer fucking skull? Ye're just throwing money down the drain.

I got three, you get three.

You cannay even choose one never mind three, fuck sake. Yeh?

Yeh fucking yeh, it's just money down the drain, fucking nuts, I dont have money to spare for that kind of bullshit; you want to go ahead go ahead, just leave me out of it, why the fucking hell you got to drag me into it, gets on my fucking nerves, it does man, the way ye go on and on.

Neither he could. It was just money down the drain, fucking nuts. I didnay have money to spare for that kind of bullshit and neither did he, but if he wanted to go ahead then go ahead just leave me out it, why the fucking hell's he got to drag me in. He got on my nerves with it.

You're too mean.

Fuck off man I'm skint, I told ye.

You aint skint.

I'm fucking skint.

You are fucking mean.

I didnay bother saying nothing back at him, otherwise on and on and on and on, digging and digging, all the fucking time fucking digging. I dont know how come he was wanting to dig at me like that but he was and it was getting at me the way he done it, he knew how to do it. Sometimes I thought Dan, just open yer mouth one more time. If it wasnay so hot I would have went and sat inside the goddam fucking hut but it

28

was burning in there and if there was no air out here in there it would be even worse, fucking furnace.

My thumbnail was catching, ragged at the corner where it got tore. I bit at it, shifting the cigarette in my other hand. Dan was looking at me. I gave him a look back. I went to the tap, drank straight from the gush and it was beautiful. Ice cold. Clear as crystal. Ye dont need no fucking beer. I wiped my mouth with the sweatrag, tugged it back up round my forehead, tightening it. The sun was burning. Some jobs ye worked they gave ye a concentrated drink for the sweat ye lost but no this one. They gave ye sweet fuck all on this one, piece of shit, they gave ye nothing; that was what they gave ye, they wanted to see that sweat; they werent happy till that sweat was running out yer whole goddam fucking body, them watching it and counting the fucking drops. Fucking bloodsuckers, a gang of fucking bloodsuckers, leeches.

McBain came out a door. He was kidding on he didnay see us, kidding on he wasnay looking. What's up, I said, we're no supposed to get a fucking food-break, hey?

You dont need no food-break, you dont eat no fucking food.

I watched McBain disappear back where he came. He's a spy that cunt.

No he aint.

Why's he watching us?

He aint no fucking spy.

You take it from me.

I dont take nothing from you.

He's a fucking spy man.

Yeh?

He fucking is, yeh.

Then how come he likes you?

He likes me!

How come?

He doesnay fucking like me man what ye talking about?

He likes you.

Yeh?

You know it.

He's got a fucking ancestor.

I got a fucking ancestor, we all fucking got ancestors.

You've no got nay fucking ancestors man.

I got ancestors.

Well so have I.

How come he gives you all the work then?

He gives you the work as well.

It's you he likes. It's you he likes Raymond. If he's a spy!

Fucking bullshit man. What ye looking at?

You.

Ye're looking at me!

Yeh.

Yeh?

Talk about it.

Talk about what?

Something nagging at you.

Is there fuck.

Talk about it.

Dan I dont want to fucking talk about fuck all. I dont want to talk about fucking nothing, okay.

What's wrong?

Fuck all, nothing, there's nothing wrong, nothing wrong fucking goddam fucking bullshit nothing, there aint fuck all wrong with me Dan there's something wrong with you but, all the time fucking nagging it's you that's fucking nagging at me man ye're like an old fucking woman. What ye looking at? Aint nothing fucking wrong Dan you listening to what I'm saying? I'm saying to you there aint fuck all fucking wrong with me.

Why you shouting?

I'm no shouting. I'm no shouting.

Yeh you are.

He looked at me then looked back at the newspaper. I finished the cigarette and flicked it away, lifted the top slice of bread to see what the hell she was giving me now. Some kind of pork roll, something, chopped ham maybe; with mustard spread thick. I closed it up and got the tin of milk, tipped it into the tea and gave it a good shake, seeing the trails and twirls. That cream she got always made them. I saw him looking at the food. He always had things different; lumps of meat. Then some fruit; his missis gave him fruit. Or his girls, they gave him it, that's who. Healthy food, he got healthy food. He made a play of that. That was how he kept his strength. Bullshit. I could fucking lose him. Anytime. Fuck him, I could leave him trailing.

Now I got that smell in my nostrils again. No good asking him. I was getting it all the time and it was like dead rats, that was what I was smelling. Ye sure ye dont smell nothing?

I dont smell nothing, I told you that. What you mean?

There's a smell, fucking dead rats, mouldy shit.

Dead rats!

That's what the smell is.

There aint no goddam smell Raymond it's your nose.

It aint my nose at all man it isnay my fucking nose.

It's your old body then, you getting decayed.

I know what it is man it's that fucking meat you're eating, what is that corpses? is that corpses you're eating? what's that woman feeding you now! fucking corpses? she been down that fucking morgue again!

She aint feeding me that, that what you're eating.

That's pork.

31

Yeh.

Pork, yeh.

And mustard.

Mustard, yeh.

That mustard, it gets cardboard tasting good.

Yeh that's right, she gets it sent special, it's fucking highclass fucking stuff.

I took a bite of a sandwich and drank some of the tea, it was sweet tasting. See this tea, I said, it's fucking beautiful, it cures a thirst.

He wasnay drinking tea, he had stopped it. He went back to the newspaper, studying through the racing. He could study at it for hours. It still done him no fucking good. Know something? I said. Hey Dan . . .

What?

I wish I was someplace else.

Yeh, like where.

Fucking anywhere, anywhere ye can breathe. Anywhere but here. Anywhere but fucking here man this job piece of shit.

You pining for something?

Pining, what ye talking about?

It's Friday.

I know what day it is. Yeh, laugh.

Raymond you somebody to laugh at.

Yeh? Well what the fuck ye think you are?

You betting them horses?

I told ye.

Get three.

Fuck off.

I got three. We'll get that big lucky going.

Big fucking unlucky.

Nothing ventured.

Dan I've got no money; how many times have I got to fucking tell ye?

You aint got no money? It's Friday. How come you aint got no money hey you dont spend nothing. Come on, you pick three. We walk out of here we'll be millionaires. The big six is lucky for us.

You want to give them yer cash, is that it?

I'll give them my cash.

That's what ye'll do then.

That's what I'll do.

Yeh, well, good, fucking go ahead.

The big six is lucky for us. You pay me later Raymond dont worry about it. Your old woman coming? Hey?

Yeh. Yeh she's coming. So what?

You can pay me later. Monday, that's okay.

Yeh!

Course you can.

It's that goddam fucking cheque Dan ye know what like it is.

Pay me Monday. Pay me Monday Raymond. Or Sunday.

Monday, we in Sunday?

Yeh.

McBain tell ye?

No he didnt tell me.

So how d'ye fucking know?

I know.

Yeh you know, yeh.

I know.

You know fucking everything dont ye. Ye're a fucking know-all that's what you are, a fucking know-all. You know everything, every goddam fucking thing. Who're ye looking at?

You.

Me?

You.

Dont fucking look at me.

Something nagging at you.

What ye talking about?

Something nagging at you Raymond.

There's fucking nothing fucking nagging at me. You're what's nagging at me.

Talk about it.

He kept on looking at me. I waited him out. He went back reading the paper again, drinking his juice. Yeh, I could wait him out. I knew the way he went. Okay, I said, so what ye eating the day?

Food.

Yeh food, it's got a smell to it. Let me see.

It's lamb.

That isnay lamb man that's fucking mutton. Dead rats, that's what that is. So how come you dont drink tea nowadays anyway hey? How come?

I told you.

Yeh but how come?

You drink it.

Yeh I drink it, you used to drink it. How come ye changed?

I changed.

Yeh how come? Who says ye were to change? yer kids?

My kids!

Yeh it was, I know it was.

You know nothing.

Ha.

It wasnt you Raymond, that is for sure.

It was yer girls, they told ye.

They didn't tell me. It wasnt my girls.

Who was it then? Ye saw it on a television programme?
Fuck you.
You read it in a magazine!
This is apple juice boy, it is pure and is unadulterated.
It'll turn yer insides into a goddam fucking orchard, all trees and branches, that's what ye'll be, yer insides, trees and branches.
Trees and branches! Where d'you get them?
Where do I get them? The same place you get your goddam fucking tool. Yeh. You heard. Ye want to know what's nagging me that's what's nagging me, how come ye got that fucking tool, you always get it!
Early bird.
Early bird. You sleep on the job man that's how, you kip up on that fifth floor. Ye dont go fucking home at night man that's how ye get it, ye fucking sleep here! Yeh, laugh.
I'll laugh.
Laugh yer fucking head off.
I'm laughing.
Yeh.
Raymond you cant walk up that fifth floor, you got to wait till they put in the elevator, you're waiting for that day; they're giving you a oxygen bottle!
Yeh, I'll strap it round my fucking back, I'll fucking fly up, I'll save up and buy a fucking aeroplane.
That's what you'll need, them cigarettes, I told you.
You told me yeh you fucking told me.
I told you.
What time's it?
I told you okay.
What time is it?
Ten minutes.
Fuck off.

35

Ten minutes.

Ten minutes . . .

Eat your food.

I'll fucking eat yours.

You want some?

Fucking corpses man ye kidding me on! Yeh, laugh, laugh.

I'll laugh.

Yeh you'll laugh. Yeh.

Raymond you're something to laugh at.

Yeh, well, laugh at this, laugh at this, her brother, I didnay tell ye – serious Dan, listen, I was gony tell ye and I forgot, it's her brother – so he comes over last weekend, him and his missis, Saturday past; so him and me, we're having a few drinks; he brung this bottle of nice brandy ye know so we're sitting, I've got the window wide open and we're sitting and he's telling me about his boys, them nephews ye know, crazy fuckers, he's talking about them, and it comes to me that he's gony die; nay kidding Dan just right out the blue it come, I saw it in him, I just fucking saw it in him, sure as fuck, like he was my own brother; we were just sitting there, and when I looked at him. I just saw it man ye know, I just saw it. Nay kidding ye.

What does that mean like he was your own brother?

I just saw it in him.

What does that mean Raymond? like he was your own brother.

I fucking saw it in him, that's what I'm saying. He was looking away and just sitting there. I just saw it. It come right out the blue to me, right there.

Dan drank down his juice and he snapped the can and chipped it at the oildrum.

So what ye got to say about that? Ye got nothing to say?

I got nothing to say.

Ho!

I dont hear you Raymond.

Ye dont hear me because ye dont fucking listen I told ye and ye dont listen.

You told me shit, I know what you told me.

I told ye something and ye didnay listen.

I listened. I listened to you.

Yeh you listened.

I done nothing but listen.

Yeh.

I'm tired of listening. I am tired of it. Fucking shit.

It aint shit.

Why you ever come here, this place? Tell me.

Ye know why.

Tell me.

The same as you, work and money.

Work and money? Is that why you come? Work and money, you come for work and money? That's what you're telling me?

Fucking work and fucking money.

That's what you come for?

That's what I come for.

There aint none. Raymond there aint none. Why you dont go home now? Go home, go fucking home.

What ye talking about?

Money and work you talking about, there aint fucking none of that boy there aint none. Hey? You dont know that? You dont fucking know there aint none? Hey? Nobody never tell you? You aint found out that one little thing?

Me? Dont talk about me, it's you, it's fucking you aint found it out man it's you. Yeh laugh. You dont fucking know it man it's you, that's your problem. Yeh laugh yer goddam fucking head off, it's you, you've just heard the news. When did ye find out?

Why dont you go home?

Why dont you?

You know why.

Yeh I know why.

Yeh you know why.

Well I cannay go fucking home either.

Yeh you can.

Can I fuck man it's past.

It's not past.

It's past. Dan it's past.

Yeh?

Ye dont know.

What dont I know.

Ye think ye do but ye dont, ye fucking dont.

Yeh?

Dan fuck sake d'ye know what age I am?

Yeh.

No ye dont. Ye dont.

I know what age you are.

Naw ye dont.

I know.

You know fuck all.

I know fuck all.

Yeh ye're laughing yeh, laugh.

What is that now I cant get laughing!

Laugh all ye fucking want, I dont give a fuck.

Raymond dont give a fuck.

That's right, goddam fucking right man I dont give a fuck, not about you, not about this fucking job piece of shit, nothing; I dont give a goddam fucking one fuck. Yeh you're laughing. One of these days . . . that's all.

38

What shit you talking now?

You heard.

I heard you shouting at me

It's you should've got the fuck out of here man no me. When you got the chance. I never got the chance you did, so why didnt ye take it, why didnt ye go? Hey, you tell me? Ye had the fucking chance man and ye didnay take it. I remember, yeh, I remember.

Raymond you know.

I know, yeh, I fucking know all right.

What you talking about?

You know what I'm talking about, you had the chance but ye didnay take it. Yeh. Know why, cause ye were too fucking feart man that's what ye were, ye were too feart! Dont talk to me! Dont fucking talk to me!

You're shouting.

I'm no shouting.

You're shouting. What's wrong with you?

I'm no fucking shouting.

Yeh you are.

Am I fuck.

You are, telling me you're dying and all this now about what you're saying; shouting at me, why're you shouting at me? Why you doing that? What's wrong with you Raymond? Hey? What's wrong with you?

I didnay tell ye I was gony die.

That's what you told me.

Did I fuck, I didnay, that's you no listening. It's her brother. You think I'm talking about myself? Bullshit Dan if ye think that, if it was me, I'd tell ye if it was me. Why would I lie about something like that? Fuck sake. Why would I lie about that?

Cause you know why? Cause you're fucking foolish, that's why. Yeh. Look what you done to your food!

My food, it's my fucking food.

Look what you done!

It's my fucking food.

You've crushed it, look, the dough's coming out the holes in your fingers. Look at that shit.

It's mustard.

You pulped them Raymond, you pulped them sandwiches.

Yeh I pulped them, I pulped them, so what? My fucking sandwiches.

I held up my hand and licked at it. That bread was soft as putty. I wiped the rest off and washed it at the tap, drank some water, got another smoke. He was watching me when I sat back down.

Why you start that smoking again?

Why d'you quit the tea?

Health.

Laugh, yeh, health, health. It's no health.

What it is then?

It's no fucking health.

So tell me Raymond, what?

It's no fucking health.

Tell me? Hey . . . ? You cant tell me.

I can tell ye.

You cant tell me.

Gie us peace.

You want peace?

Yeh I fucking want peace, peace from fucking you, peace from fucking everything, this fucking place bullshit shiteing fucking place piece of shit man. They give us nothing, they're sticking this goddam building up with nothing, we're doing this job for nothing, it's worth nothing, the whole goddam fucking lot, we're putting it up man it's gony fucking fall down, this whole place.

Yeh and it aint our business.

It aint our business? When we aint got the fucking tools, you're telling me that? One stupit fucking goddam fucking pipe? Yeh and you nab it. Dont talk to me about tools!

You get here first.

If I come first I still dont get it because you fucking hide it man that's what you do. Should be more than one of them.

Should be but there aint.

So where d'ye hide it? I know where ye hide it.

A secret place.

I know.

You know!

I know.

No you dont.

You go up the top of the building, where the generator's at.

Yeh that's where I go but I dont take the pipe there.

No.

I take the pipe somewheres else.

I know where you take it.

No you dont.

Yeh I do, I seen ye fucking take it there.

Where?

Where ye take it. Yeh ye're laughing.

I'm laughing, you something to laugh at.

Me. It's no me fucking eating corpses man I'll tell ye that. Lamb? That's no lamb, fucking rats man!

You want some?

Laugh, yeh, fuck you.

I got up and left him and went for a wander, down to the gate, someplace, till then it was time and now my back was sore and my knees were sore and every goddamn fucking bit of me. The strain told here at my left wrist and it felt weak.

41

And it looked weak God almighty that was the first I had ever seen it it even looked weak. I switched the hammer back on then off again, I put it down, wiped at the sweat on my neck. The sun beating down, the noise of the drilling still in my ears. Then the fucking smell again. It wasnt decaying bodies, I smelled that before one time, then we found it and that was what it was a decayed body, some poor old bastard.

The small of the spine there that's where it was, it was killing me. The hammer was no fucking good, it had no pressure, I had to put in the force myself, it was like a pipsqueak. I got a cigarette going. There was something up with them too, ye bought them good as gold and then ye tried to smoke them, ye couldnay, ye couldnay smoke a damn one of them. Ye couldnay get a fucking drag, no the way ye used to. It was like they had done some extraction job on the fucking nicotine, that was what it was like, they had extracted out the fucking tobacco and did some kind of substitution job, cotton wool.

I sat down on the planks, keeping to the side of the scaffolding. I wasnt worried about getting spotted. I done the work, they knew that.

I hadnay seen the ganger since before the break, Stansfield, I knew where he was, alki bastard, I seen where he went.

A nice cold beer. I wouldnay have taken one myself. I could have. But I wouldnay. Not now and not later and not no other damn time. Even if I could have walked off the fucking job. I still wouldnay have. All that good money getting pissed down the drain, there was no point to it. It wasnay something ye could look forward to, not any more. Yeh sure in the old days, I wouldnay deny it, a few beers. But no now, no with them arsehole bastards, each time ye stepped round the corner, no-good scratching bastards, they didnay leave ye alone. Wanting to work? They werenay wanting to work. Then ye gave them something and ten minutes later there they were back in at ye. One time I was there working and what do ye know two of them, they were in through the gate bold as fuck, me and Dan unloading a wagon, and them cunts are over and trying for a coin. Me and him, working there, them arsehole bastards, we couldnay believe it, fucking wagonful of fucking cement.

I leaned my forehead against a drum for a second. It was cool. It was surely cool.

Then when me and her went off a holiday it would be winter, where the hell could we go? We could go somewhere, we would get away, maybe down the coast, go see the sea, just walk, smell that sweet saltwater, me and her. There wasnay nothing wrong with me it was the entire place was no good, never been nothing else. Maybe I was getting old but that was what it seemed like. Ye looked at that skyline and ye wanted the fuck out, where's the mountains, I hadnay seen a goddam fucking mountain, for how long, I was gony go crazy, hellhole, that was what it was, if I didnay get out, I knew it, knew it for sure, like it was itching inside of me, that was what it was, that was what it was like Jesus God, crawling around, I could feel it there and it was long and slinky goddam covered in hairs and fur, slithering down there inside my guts, that was where it lived. Dan telt me about this other fellow, black fellow, come from Africa, and he used to say something, they would be on the job and Dan here trying to get him to slow down, sit for a spell, and the other fellow would, but ten seconds and he would be jumping up from where he was sitting and then he would say it in his own tongue and Dan didnay know what the goddam hell it was and when he asks him the fellow says, Look boy ye sits too long on that same spot one of them old centipedes come out and he crawls up yer arse. That was what the fellow telt him.

43

McBain was there now. I took a last drag on the cigarette and chipped it, slung the line across my shoulder and footered with the nozzle, like I was adjusting it, some damn thing, what did it matter. He didnay mind too much; I done the business, he knew me. I triggered a couple of blasts for good measure and moved to where I was working, then to inside the building, getting on with the finishing work for the electrical boxes. Dan was way above. I could hear him, sometimes he didnay stop, probably tied down the fucking trigger, getting the feet up, wily bastard. In the old days ye would have swung the sledge and nobody the wiser when ye stopped for a smoke, there wasnay nobody could tell except maybe they might have listened for the chip chip. But not this goddam hammer. Once ye stopped working they knew, they heard that silence.

The chisel was all chewed up. I screwed it back in. None of them was fit to grind a tooth. Clean strength was all that was boring them holes. I was on my knees, fixing it in, pressed the trigger, feeling the jar, then the chisel fucking stuck goddam fucking no-good thing stuck right there, wedged solid. I unscrewed it again, lifting the nozzle up, started booting at the chisel to loosen it out the concrete.

There was McBain, crept round me, the time he chose, I kicked at the chisel, stamped at it with my heel. Fuck you. He was watching me do it, I got it loosened out. The kind of job this was. They sprung out at ye.

You having trouble Raymond?

What?

He was chewing something, standing there with his hands in his pockets, staring sideways and up the building where a guy was working on a cradle. I saw my hardhat, it was lying just over the way. I went over and got it and pulled it on. He was looking roundabout like he didnay notice. Dan here? he said.

I nodded my head up the way, where the noise was.

Yeh, he said; we got a load coming in; you want to stay for it?

If ye like.

Be a couple of hours, you'll be paid through four.

Okay. I had the chisel in now and I triggered a couple of blasts.

You meeting the missis?

Yeh.

She coming to the gate?

Yeh.

I reckon about seven, a half after, that should see it.

She can come back.

You'll be paid through four.

Right.

McBain looked back up to the cradle, watching it swing out while the guy there did what he did. McBain nodded. You seen Stansfield?

No.

When you last see him?

A while.

Since the break?

Dont know.

You think Dan'll stay on?

Yeh.

It's a two-man job.

Right.

You'll tell him?

He's up on the fifth.

McBain nodded.

Yeh.

I took the call there; load's due in around five. Depending on the road. He's got to haul south then.

Yeh.

I appreciate it Ray.

Yeh. I triggered another couple of blasts, waiting for him to go. Dan had sympathy for the guy, I didnay. He stood on, looking roundabout. I just got back working.

My eldest

I was waiting for water-insects to clamber over my shoes. The myriad lurking beneath boulders, the ones with many feet, these yins that flounder on their backs when you lift up the boulder. I didnt feel sorry for them. I didnt feel anything about them at all, I was just waiting for them, or for others.

The umpteen bits of bleached crab shell.

This observing the sea; waves breaking, the little boat with its blue cockpit; the seabirds. These might be the elements, not the central elements. Life or death, shifting of water in the shallows, green, brown. It was impossible. Of course I knew things would co-exist. Their very presence, a relationship, the living. Also when ye returned a freedom. Knowing this eventually. This would cause despair. All it required was my head. I stared out from the shore.

Maybe as well as that the wide expanse. That wide expanse and the sense too of history, the old graveyard was not in view but I knew precisely where it was, the clump of trees that led to it.

I untied my shoelaces and took off my socks, stuffed them in the shoes; flung them back over my shoulder one at a time, without checking where they might fall. Pools nestled in the rocks. So could be this was a test. I used to be good at tests. Now a pair of birds with long necks were there, less than a hundred metres away, necks craning. Maybe they were *cranes*. I know almost nothing about birds except they fly up in the air. Most of them. While these two here were the kind that went skimming the surface of the water.

I took off my tee shirt and flung that back over my shoulder. It would land in a pool. Nothing was more certain. I didnt have to look. Everybody carries a certain amount of luck: it is the kind of luck, this is what matters. I knew about my luck, the kind I carried. What could be said about that. It was just something that was an essential part of me, neither good nor bad.

And there was the green yacht and the red sails down, the engine taking it out through the islands, the owners not content to look for a breeze, there was no breeze, there was always a breeze, not now there wasnt there was no breeze, nothing, the still and the quiet, the things I was seeing, everything was just so distant. It had nothing to do with me. It really did not have anything to do with me.

It was strange where you found fires. One had been here, not too far from where I was sitting; somebody maybe had brewed up, hot tea, with concentrated milk, too sweet but good, grey flecks of ash; and ash in the tea; nobody in their right mind would care, they would dig it out or spit it out and smile, and sip, make wry comments, and sip, and smile; whoever they had been, two people, maybe three. Wishing they werent vegetarians, if that was what they were, because of the smell of sausages frying on a campfire; memories of childhood.

If I swam out I wouldnt drown. Unless a hopeless cramp, unless hitting some hopeless undercurrent. Things that were hopeless.

A mild wave breaking, more of them. Some boat away way out, a big boat. And a whooping, I heard a whooping. My kids, three of them, two boys and a wee lassie, the youngest. I sat there on the boulder, they came running behind me. My back and my shoulders. The back of my skull; their dad in a reverie, staring into the sea. I carried this beyond a limit so they became silent after the first shouts. Why was I doing it? It was intentional. The eldest was in my line of vision but I was as if I didnt care if I saw him or not. I sensed about him that he was trying hard not to be uneasy, not to be frightened maybe, by me. The wee yin had found my shoes.

My wife would have followed them down the rocky path to the shore. If I turned I would see her breaking her way out through the bushes.

What did I feel like christ, was I dreaming? The wee yin spoke to me and I answered her without knowing what it was about. Then behind her I saw the big boy and I knew I definitely was frightening him and I said, It's okay son what's up? and I reached out my hand and grasped his wrist.

His brother was there as well and saying, I was wanting to show ye something dad.

Fine son nay bother.

Here's yer tee shirt, he said and when I smiled so did he. And the wee lassie said: Dad are you gon to swim?

Yip.

She laughed, You're silly.

I am, yeh.

Now my wife was here and she was not able to avoid the smile, wiping out the previous bad feeling, the kids showing her my clothes and chattering away. Ye arent gon to swim? she said.

Yep.

Ye'll glow in the dark.

It's daylight.

She looked at me, then said: Dont, it's mad.

I want to sit on a trident submarine.

Sit on top of it? said my daughter.

Ower the top of it. I just feel like swimming ower the top of it, yeh, that's what I feel like doing.

49

I saw my eldest boy standing there and I winked, but he was tense, so tense. Come here son, I said, but he stayed put. I reached my hand out to him. It's alright, I said, come here. But he turned and ran off across the pebbles and boulders.

It happened to me once

That way ye are with a hangover and this guy behind me in the queue: Some fags seem to last forever, he says, I'm talking about roll-ups, but only them ones ye dont have to keep lighting all the time, the ones that burn of their own free-will.

I wasnay in the best of conditions, being honest, and it took a minute for it to reach me. Even then but I wasnay sure if I had heard right. The way he was standing he was a bit to my side; I knew he was watching me out the corner of his eye. This being London too that made it worse, ye're trying to keep a low profile. Eventually I gave him a look. Instead of shutting up he said, It's totally crazy how it happens.

How what happens?

Naw just what I was saying there.

I dont know what ye were saying there.

I only mean if ye let them, that's what I mean. Ye dont have to let them but, ye can make sure they go out. Mind you there's nothing guaranteed. If ye let them last they'll last forever.

Jesus christ.

It's a point of view. Everybody's entitled to that.

Are they? Fucking world do you live in? I said, Ye're talking shite.

Which should have brought an end to the conversation but it didnay. Because I had smiled when I said it. I wasnay sure if I was talking to a genuine idiot and it was that way ye get feeling sorry for somebody, but because he had got

me to smile that was him; he rolled up his newspaper like
he was all set to leave, never mind he was about thirty-third
in the queue. He spoke again and this time his voice was
loud and clear:

What I'm saying is there's some roll-ups ye can spend yer
life relighting – cause they'll never end, okay, fair enough
– but there's them other yins and ye dont. Usually what
happens is ye think they've gone out, but they havenay, as
soon as ye gie them a couple of puffs that's that, ye're back
smoking again. Ye have to toss them away, dump them into
a fucking puddle, know what I mean, otherwise ye'll never
get rid of them.

I dont smoke, I says, but if I did ye'd get fuck all.

He squinted at me. I squinted back at him. D'ye think I'm
trying to tap ye! he said, smiling.

I dont care.

I'm no trying to tap ye.

Aye well ye would get fuck all if ye were, I dont even
smoke.

Now he looked this way and that, still smiling, like he
couldnay believe the line I was taking with him. I wondered
if I knew him from somewhere, but I didnay, no from Adam.
Stupid bastard, was he trying to take the piss?

He carried on talking. What happens at the wind up, he
says, ye have to fling them away because they begin to gie
ye the heave. Speaking personally I've never hung about till
the end, I usually get scunnered long before that. It's like my
entire body and brain's got sickened. Honest, just cause of
that one fag.

So how come ye dont just leave it on the ashtray and
smoke it later? How come ye dont just smoke it the rest of
yer fucking life and save yerself a fortune?

Now he gave a wee shake of the head. It's no as simple as

that pal, ye're talking generally and it never happens generally. Ye can watch and wait all ye like but ye dont notice, no till it's too late. Ye think these thoughts but they aye vanish as soon as ye have them, they go right out yer head. Take it from me, ye just cannay hold onto them. The number of times I've thought of something. Then it disappears. And that's forever as well. Ye think nothing lasts but it doesnay last forever so that means it does last, just the fact it doesnay. Smoking's different. You're no a smoker anyway, I can tell.

Ye can tell because I telt ye.

Naw, I would have known it without that.

He shook his head like he was talking to a mug. Maybe it was because I wear specs. Some folk think it is a sign ye are a fucking mug. It was one of the problems in this part of the city as well, ye never knew who was at yer back. For all I fucking knew he had a weapon in his pocket. That way ye go all tense. I thought I could hear him muttering or else sniggering. I wished I knew how many people were behind me in the queue but I didnay and there was nay way I was turning round. That would just have gave him the opportunity. There was nay smell of drink aff him either. Maybe he was stoned. Lucky bastard! But how come it was me, it was aye me, I aye got fucking cornered by crackpots, it was like they followed me about, they waited there till I stepped out the close. Here he comes! I could imagine them nudging each other. Here he comes! probably they paid a couple of bob into a kitty. That was to get me. Else I was fucking raffled. Top prize. This morning's fucking halfwit. That was what I was, a fucking halfwit. What was I doing what was I doing? With my life, my fucking life. What was I standing here for? this fucking place, a den of iniquity. What was I gony do after it? I knew the walk I had to do inside out, even to get started I had to go down this long big avenue that

53

drove ye fucking crackers, ye looked up and saw it stretching,
it took ye fucking ages. And then when I got to the boulevard.
And from there to where I was gon.

For fuck sake.

I was losing the place.

I shut my eyes and kept them shut. What if I fainted? There
was two black guys in front of me, one with dreads. I would
land on top of them. I had to sort myself out. I opened my eyes
and started looking about like I was seeing things of interest,
noting them down in my mind's eye – just fucking anything,
I stared at it as if I was taking it all in. I was a bundle of
nerves but and it wasnay working. Why me, why fucking
me. The queue moved up a couple of places but needless
to say he was still behind me. Where else would he be. I
kept my head to the front. Then he started again like we
knew each other and used to be close mates or something.
The tone of his voice made me turn round, I couldnay stop
myself, just something.

It's only a habit, he said, we've all got habits; that's one of
mine's. It's no as interesting as some but who knows.

Who knows, I says, ya fucking halfwit.

He smiled. Even with me saying what I had said he still
smiled. And I thought to myself ya cunt ye you've got
nay fucking nerves, ye might have nay brains but ye've
got nay fucking nerves either.

Then I knew he was waiting, he was fucking waiting. I
knew it. Well I wasnay taking nay fucking chances, no with
a cunt like that.

I telt myself to relax, cool it, fucking cool it, ye're jumpy as
fuck, the way it's gon if that fucking clerk says the wrong word
ye're gony get done for grievous body. No way I thought, no
way, I'm no getting fucking done for nay cunt, no him no
fucking naybody. I turns and says, Look I'm no wanting nay

trouble here, we've all got problems. I'm skint too, right, I'm skint, I am fucking skint. Know what I mean?

Take it easy pal.

Aye take it easy aye.

And now what I noticed was his voice was growling. You're from up the road, he says, so am I. Eh?

Eh what.

We're baith frae up the road?

Aye.

I didnay know that when I started to talking to ye. I didnay. Eh? ye hear me?

Aye I fucking hear ye aye, what ye saying?

He smiled.

What ye smiling for?

There's a time to fuck off, he said, this is it.

I saw one of the black guys taking out a stick of chewing gum and I felt like asking him for a bit, it was like a life-saver, getting somebody else into the conversation.

When ye think about it the place was mobbed and there I was on my tod, me and me alone, I me myself.

Fucking jonah, nemesis, whatever. It went through my heid what he had said, there's a time to fuck off. He was right. I knew he was right, he was fucking dead right. Then it happened I was wanting to shake his hand but I couldnay do that either, no in the off-chance. So I kept my back to him. I heard a noise, I wasnay sure if it was his feet were shuffling. Crunch time. I knew it was fucking coming. I thought to myself, what age are ye now? How far have ye fucking got!

The Norwest Reaches

My body was responding to the cold in a series of uncontrolled chitters. One need not travel to the Arctic wastes. Stalactites hung from the top of the bedroom window. Never mind the glass all frosted, the dampness iced over, the poor old fungus having to revitalise itself in combat against this early February morning. And here was my wife, her eyes closed, nestling beneath the cosy luxury of the quilt. Come on, I urged, I'm a virile man, let me back in!

My breath was steaming, I was in slow motion, I blew steam-circles, my jaw muscles jerking. Meanwhile her head vanished and I was pulling on my socks when she reappeared, hand on dressing-table so not to lose balance. And her most sultry tones, whispering: Get back in here!

Too late woman.

Come on . . . She patted my place beside her, a form of invitation always arriving too late, too late. Come on . . .

If ye're serious I wish I could but I cannot, I have to go to work.

Her smile altered. No ye dont. And leaning her head on the palm of her hand she drew back the quilt, exposing the sheet in the halflight, the beauty of her shoulders, the softness I knew so well.

Temptress, I have a job of work.

It's not a real job of work.

But it was a real enough occupation. I was on my way ben the kitchenette where I prepared tea, then into the little dinette to see how things were on the southern reaches,

carefully, so not to awaken the infant, parting the curtains at the day beyond, not even a bleak watery sun. No damn sun. Fiercely cold I reckoned. I have become adept at gauging the atmosphere through glass, estimating the temperature to a reasonable degree. When asked Is it cold outside? I could glance out that window and reply Yes, wrap up.

I switched on the fire in the living room and brrrrrd, brrrrrd, rubbing my upper arms, watching the sparks fly at the corners of the knackered electric bar. All the same I was knackered myself and collapsed onto the fireside chair.

I really was knackered. It was like I could not move, not a muscle. What was happening to me? Was it merely fatigue? Was I sickening? How could that be? Unless I was coming down with the flu or some related virus. People were complaining of assorted ailments many of which offered a consistency, and people could not be avoided; I was out there amongst them.

A shawl. It had come to us from my wife's grandmamma. Now it lay over the back of the sofa. I pulled it to, and over myself. It was great.

That was a thing of course the baby. How long had it been since last I had a full eight-hour sleep? Uninterrupted sleep; just lying from half eleven right the way through, right until that rising moment. And of course my wife.

But this chittering I was doing! I held the shawl tight about me, drew my feet up on the chair, curled myself into a bundle, my shoulders shuddering. Now I could enjoy everything, most particularly the shift in body-temperature. Oh dear! I closed my eyes. The next thing it was ten past nine and my feet were in a hell of a state, itchy and sore, too close to that fire, the old chilblains acting up. No work today. I heard banging noises and smiled. My wife was out and about, she was at the sink. She would not have to fill a kettle since

inside lay my water, unused. Through the dinette door I saw the baby, now in the highchair, gurgling ten to the dozen, trying to stand, clawing upwards to the very stars. I held the shawl about my shoulders, struggling up from the armchair, stumbling my way through on those sensitive stocking-soles, giving my wife a wave at the kitchenette doorway. Ye're awake, she said, yes – we need bread and milk. Bread and milk! I spoke to her directly. See when I die, I said but was unable to finish the sentence, the baby having laughed.

When ye die? said my wife. Uhuh, yes, go on!

Naw but honestly my dear I'll be happy to expire, no two ways about it. I'll savour it, *the* expiration.

We'll all savour it.

The moment of extinction, a sharp clap of the hands, the obverse of creation.

In front of the baby?

In front of any baby. The satisfaction of an inference made soundly, that baby will be replete. Such filial information is to be imparted honestly. It's good that a baby should know these things, we should not withhold strong realities from the next generation. Parents must try to adopt new ways, different ways, we have to transmit proper information. I intend a new beginning.

After yer death?

My death is a part thereof.

I quite agree.

But go and get the milk . . . !

And the bread, she said, we need bread too.

I kept the shawl round myself.

We need bread too.

Another thing, I said, I've become an unbalanced person, my movements seem to be normal but they arent. Being a father is a natural occupation but the minutiae themselves

are unnatural, we have to fight clear from these basic contradictory premises, if they arent contradictory the least way
they are in opposition, thus we are in conflict, from the very
moment of conception.

My wife smiled. Get the milk.

March is a good month let me tell you. And it follows
from this one. It may well be cold but it heralds the new. It
contains thirty-one days and also the start of the Flat season.
It is a time when one takes stock of the present with regard
to career-prospects and a fulfilled life: the trapper leaves
the homestead and heads for the norwest reaches, kayak
on head, breaking the ice as he goes, wielding the trusty
musket, the hook, line and sinker, the varied traps for the
varied game. The mothers collect the berries, singing songs
redolent of the waulking tradition, learned at the breasts of
their mothers. Breasts.

Never you mind breasts. Since ye're here ye're here. We
need the bread and the milk.

I know I know, my feet are killing me, these blasted
chilblains, if you hadnt let me sleep! They got roasted.

I didnt let ye sleep I didnt even know ye were still here.
Since ye are still here we need milk, milk and bread.

I'm going I'm going. But I went to her first and we
cuddled. My wife was as soft and her shape as right, as fitting.
I manoeuvred to reach behind with my hand, back towards
the baby, lest she be excluded from our embrace. The shawl
had fallen from my shoulders. We clung together. Ohhh, my
wife said, it's so much better when you dont go to work.

I know, I know. I picked the shawl from the floor, folded
it over the cot, kissed the baby on the forehead. Okay wee
wummin, see ye later; twenty minutes at the most. Daddy is
not going to work today.

I pulled on my boots and got on my heavy winter jacket. I

bade cheerio, then down the stairs and out the close, cutting along through the rear and down the adjacent street. The frost bit on weeds and parked motor cars, these little zigzag blocks of it, like a cankerous growth. A neighbour was in the shop. When he saw me he shivered. How's it going? I said.

Ohhh God!

Cold yin eh!

Phhwwhhh.

The shopkeeper looked up from the cheese while slicing off a lb chunk, he gave me a smile, dropped the chunk onto the weighing machine. It came to within a half oz of the lb. My neighbour nodded and the shopkeeper wrapped the cheese.

I'm not going to work, I told him, no traps to lay.

My neighbour had a miffed look about him. You're lucky ye've a job to go to.

Och, I said, it was never a real job, imagine a real job, being a hunter in Labrador for instance, that must be something. The ice there is so deep it's blue, it's way deeper than the green ye might expect, it's beyond anything.

The shopkeeper was reserving his smile, but he didnt succeed. It was for his benefit I had made the comment. Now in response he said to my neighbour: The base of an iceberg can be the size of Scotland.

I smiled. We two had a rapport. Like myself he took an interest in the big big world, the wide wide world. If it was only the two of us in the shop we could blether for hours. The shopkeeper's wife would peer out from the curtain that separated the rear of the premises; the kitchen, wherein she fried sausage, bacon and eggs for hungry wayfarers and workers.

When my wife's waters broke it was the shopkeeper did the donkey work with emergency call-outs. One of his favourite books was a biographical work concerning a famous Chinese hunter of the earlier 20th century who trapped the icebound wastes of the far north provinces. The shopkeeper loaned the book to me but I found the translation cumbersome.

He laughed loudly at that. Never mind the translation! What about the story? What about the man himself? Did ye see the photograph? That's a real photograph! What did ye make of the furs he wore? Ye see how much fat he carried? He was no skinny-malinky, he couldnt afford to be, all his provisions and weaponry! that guy was a walking cargo-container. How else would he have survived!

The shopkeeper laughed again, a beautiful mocking laugh, beginning against me but ending with an ironic shake of his head on observing his own hands, engaged in one of their many practised tasks. Now lapsing into silence, and several moments passing, and his cheery wee whistle now starting, yeh, now it started.

That was the sort of man he was. It was always a pleasure to enter his shop. Often my wife wondered where I had got to, had I got lost.

I was asking a question too

Here was this long novel I was given to read where the action stops and the writer starts discussing questions to do with life and death, existence. It was peculiar the way it connected with me. Everything he was saying seemed like déjà vu, then almost predictable. I felt like throwing the book away. Then I picked out another couple of books and looked into them and there it was, the same again. I began to feel better. I got led into further exploration. Wisdom about wisdom. Being wise about being wise. There was nothing unusual about this; I always liked listening to conversations where folk carried on in a high intellectual style. It wasnt pretentious of me I dont think. But it was only later it came to mean something real. Not at first because it took so long. What I was doing was quite hard going and people usually have to go to university. It was all quite ironic but I couldnt have cared less. The fact of the matter is that I *didnt* care about myself, let alone anybody else. All that scrambling that goes on between people was just too ludicrous. I was at the stage where you cannot help but notice, even if you question yourself doing it you cannot stop it, not once you've got there, to that point. I had reached it. At the same time it was impossible to treat what I was doing seriously. Well what I was doing was serious but me doing it, this is what seemed a bit ridiculous, there was a nonsensical thing about it. Saying this to myself reminded me of a close friend who was dead but before he died, when he was ill, he would come out with little phrases that used to baffle the nurses. I used to nod like I understood. He didnt know I was doing it; at this time in his illness he didnt know who I was. When I sat beside his bed he would look at me occasionally, being curious, but he wasnt curious enough to take it any further. After his death I moved elsewhere, just anywhere I felt drawn. I let whims lead me. I didnt want to talk about it, about myself, about what was upsetting me. I didnt even think I was upset but no doubt I was. I had to have been. He wasnt my 'lover' or anything like that, it wasnt that kind of relationship; besides, he was a lot older. There was a couple of people where I worked, I might have spoken to them, but I had lost the energy. That time was finished. I managed to carry on working in the place but I kept myself to myself. In the past I used to blurt things out, private details; it just finished by screwing me up, and then it could get you into misunderstandings. The trouble here was that if I didnt get to talk it out with somebody then I wouldnt know how it was going, except if maybe I could sense it.

This is why I started doing what I did, helping myself to get through that bad period of uncertainty. I stuck things up on the wall, things from the books I was reading, pithy little sayings and . . . just statements; but sometimes they were hard going, a lot of them were. But some of them left me gawking in astonishment. They could get me so high I had to shut the book and walk about the floor for a while, then going back later and seeing if they still held it for me. I pinned a couple on the kitchen door. That was an old habit but then it had been messages to myself about things needing to be done. Maria from next door noticed and made ironic comments. I wasnt bothered. One time we had a sort of sex together but it didnt go further. Drunken fumblings. I made a later attempt but it was half-hearted, I didnt think she was really interested. She had a great imagination and it took her to other planes. I tried to reach these planes. She was a stronger reader than me and in this she reminded me of someone else. Some of the books she liked were well beyond me and I could hardly understand some of the things she spoke about although they did make a kind of sense while she was saying them. Then later it all evaporated and I wondered where it had gone. I had been trying the writers she spoke about and they were difficult and I couldnt understand much although the occasional thing bore in to me. Even some of these I couldnt understand, not truly. But I pinned them up on the wall. It was a mistake though because it came to be like they were making a fool of me, the way they stared me in the face, the ends of the paper curling up and the hard lump of blu-tack underneath. I remember Maria was out on the landing mending a fuse and the thought of her body made me smile. She wore jeans and they had empty bulges at the knees. Mine did too. So they should have had me smiling. But they didnt. My own trousers I found ridiculous but not amusing, not amusing; and not ordinary. Maria you're always mending things, I said, some people would take you for the landlord.

Not you.

No not me.

Anyway, our landlord doesnt mend a single bloody thing, he lets everything slide.

I watched her unscrewing the nails in the light switch. With her around you didnt have the need to rush into talk. All the same I preferred to talk. This is the mood I was in. I told her I was writing into notepads nowadays, there was so much new information to digest.

So you're still reading?

Of course.

And you're still being bamboozled?

Of course.

I listened to her breathing. She knew I was still standing there and probably she was searching for something to say; then she came out with: Is there no space left on your walls?

Dont be so sarcastic.

Well it can be a mistake to think of reading in that way. It's a mistake made by many people; you dont want to be one of them

Why not?

You dont.

How would you know what I want?

She acted like she hadnt heard me. She was cutting little ends off the wires and then was inserting them into the switch. I left her and went downstairs and she called after me: Patience is a virtue.

She was somebody to talk. Why couldnt she just leave things alone? Of course it was right what she said because I was always impatient. People have criticised me for this from time immemorial. It never ever bothered me. I was quite pleased to be seen as 'impatient'. It meant I was seen with a way of looking at the world that was slightly different from other people; otherwise why tell me.

I thought of my brain absorbing things like a sponge; later I would squeeze the sponge out. But there was no guarantee this new information would not simply emerge in its elemental drips and drops, not formed into anything, it would just be disjointed, disturbing.

There is far too much information to digest. Even when a book is very thin, it still has much that is hard to take. People are no different from books. When I thought of Maria I just smiled. Soon she would have a manfriend, I knew the signs.

Although there could be a beautiful clearness about what

65

I was reading there were times I became queasy. This might happen when I picked up from where I had left off the day or night previously. I tried picking out sentences and statements at random. It was this brought forth 'versailintude'. Later I discovered lo and behold it was not versailintude but 'verisimilitude'. I had made a mistake when writing the word down. It was a funny sort of mistake to make. I seemed to have got so engrossed in the sense behind it that the word had become my own and I took it down out of my own head instead of from the actual page where I found it. But I left it in the notepad in the mistaken spelling because here it was a new word altogether and I studied the writings of somebody else altogether because here it was something I connected with out of the mistake, and almost like how could it be a mistake if it was my very own, and why not just a new creation altogether?

I set all this into the notepad. Needless to say religion was not part of my thoughts although you might have thought so.

But then too a new thing was happening. I could be concentrating hard on my copying then when I got to the mid-point in a passage I discovered I didnt need to go any further because I seemed to understand it already like it was almost in advance I was doing it. But not having somebody to bounce off the idea: how could I know I had the idea properly? It was no good seeking out Maria who would only smile at me and a mystery would arise out of nothing and I didnt need any more mysteries, not from the outside. It was her way of keeping the mystery of knowledge and it was something I didnt like about her. Her smile made you think she understood what you were trying to capture but the only reason she didnt explain it to you was because she reckoned the act of unravelling the mystery could only take place in the pursuit. And in this she reminded me of the person I was close to and who died.

For all I knew the thing I grasped didnt exist anywhere except inside my own head. The thought that the writer was trying to communicate to me wasnt the thought I got when reading his actual words. But the words themselves were a translation because his original words, the language he wrote in, was not my language. So the thought communicated to me, where had it come from? It could be a mistaken thought. But a mistaken thought is also a thought and could not be anything other and was a part of the whole baggage.

When I got back to my room I heard movement from outside the door; it was a pair of step-ladders. Maria was shifting them from one place to another. I glanced at the door; there was no glass pane above it; even if she placed the step ladders on the other side she would not be able to look in and see me. One time she said that when she saw me on the street she had to blink twice because she saw the me underneath, my legs and body without the clothes, just my bare feet and legs walking. That made me laugh. It gave me an insight into the behaviour of women like her. I also had a funny notion that if ever I was a school teacher or put in charge of a bunch of children, I knew I could remain in control if they were all like her and not only like her but even if it was the wildest bunch of hardcase boys imaginable, I could still manage. That was what I thought!

All these bits and pieces, promises you didnt keep and things you said you knew but didnt, not through any fault of your own but just because you had made a mistake. Anything that couldnt make a mistake, leaving aside computers and machines since they were man-made – and animals – they had to be left aside since they didnt have any wills of their own.

Now the phone was ringing. I turned my back on the door.

The phone would not be for me. But it still rang. I was torn
between answering it and being nasty or just leaving it alone.
Maybe Maria would answer, unless she was balanced on top
of the ladder. My stomach was in knots. I was chewing on
my right knuckle again, I hadnt done that for a while. I had
this image in my mind's eye, there I was lying in bed with
the quilt over my head and somebody was staring at me but I
felt that it was all just another kind of wisdom. And if I lifted
the phone it would only be a voice. Such was the inability of
all the wisdom in the world. Always you were left high and
dry and on your lonesome. I took down the weetabix and
shoved two of them into a bowl then poured in some milk.
It was an obvious point when you knew it, but I was away
past that stage, I was a long way past it. I felt strong though.
I felt I had come out of it, it had been exorcised. But then I
wasnt so sure, I couldnt trust myself. I thought I might never
come to terms with anything ever again, and the phone was
still ringing it just would not stop.

Yeh, these stages

It dawned on me I hadnay been listening to music for a long time. Days. Quite a lot of days. That was a sign of how things had been, my psychological state. Not necessarily depressed. But maybe just out of things, on a sort of downside keel, no wind, just drifting about with the sails slack, not knowing fuck all, about what I was doing, not capable of thinking such thoughts. My partner had been gone for a while now and even going to bed was nothing to look forward to. I hadnt made the fucking thing since she left. The sheets and pillows disgusted me, the oily bit where my head lay. I wasnt washing properly, not one solitary shower in at least ten days. Falling apart! I saw myself in the typical male role, helpless without a woman, the poor wee boy syndrome. Yet this wasnay me. It was annoying to think I had let it go this far. Time to get a grip. I began in a straightforward way. I stuck on some music and let it blast out. I opened the curtains then the windows. Then I was fuckt. I sat down on the edge of the bed and felt like killing myself. It got worse, I was into the kind of despair that makes suicide a positive move. I heard somebody chapping the door. Fuck them, whoever it was.

Which wasnt my real thought. At that moment my state of mind meant this sort of thought was beyond me. I just didnt budge, mentally or physically. I was staring at the floor, wondering about something to do with certain dods of oose and fluff, I think, if they might have been unusual insects, some uncharted species, it isnay as if science knows everything or has ever discovered everything. Even living

69

organisms, some dont fucking even count; they arenay even worthy of being verified as extant, they arenay even worthy of reaching the state of the fucking dodo, an entry into an encyclopedia.

The chapping on the door, when it occurred to me that this indeed is what had happened; it took a bit of time to hit me. I wasnt capable of being there in the head at the same time the chapping was happening, I was behind the time the way it should be if you happen to be in an ordinary psychological condition, not well-being – who cares about well-being – but just an average sort of routine condition. There was a song I liked, I had been listening to, not recently, fairly recently, a couple of weeks, ten days, who knows – but it got to something, it was to do with it, the state I was in, the depth, that song was reaching down there, and it wasnt even the song it was the backing instrument, whatever the fuck it was, a box-accordion maybe, it was a depth, it was reaching some kind of depth, that way sunlight pierces right down through water, looking up and seeing it so far above, seaweed flowing by yer skalp. Needless to say by the time I opened the thing, the door, whoever it was had vanished, if somebody had been there, if at all. So this human absence there on the doorstep. I found I was scratching my bolls. I definitely needed to shower. Desperate. This human absence on the doorstep

I tried to keep the train of thought going but didnay succeed. It was just overwhelming, the state I was in. Imagine being in such a state! Christ almighty. But at least I knew it was a stage. Or I thought I did. I hoped it was. I had that hope. I turned back and I didnt want to open my door, not any further, I was not wanting to go into the room, I wasnt wanting to. I was really scared.

But it wasnay a way to be, I knew that. Fucking hell man

come on, come on, it's only yer woman's away for a few days, ye're not getting it the gether properly, that's all. I pushed open the door and saw it staring back at me, all these fucking bits and pieces; mainly they were hers, they belonged to her, but they were all out of place and topsy turvy. Come on I said be practical be practical. And there was the television. It was a magnetic force, drawing my wrist, pulling me towards it, right into it, the other world, where my world was not, I got sucked in, I could get sucked in, even now, even so, even yet: just close yer eyes, keep yer way, tacking through the debris, the fucking wash, five steps and reach and ye shall find. So that made me smile, the syntax, then the sea, the fucking sea. I was seeing the stuff now, I stepped forward and picked up an empty can of lager. It was so easy. I just reached down and lifted the fucker and squashed it, dumped it into a polybag that was lying there, I must have put it there for the purpose at some earlier time, an energetic instant. But I knew I had to watch myself and be attentive to these practical acts and not get sidetracked. There was the ashtray surrounded by ash and where was the hoover? but before that get the debris get the debris. And I replaced the bits and pieces, and then when I got into the kitchenette and saw the state of that! I just put in the stopper thing in the sink and piled in the dishes and the cutlery. Ran the tap, sprinkled the washing-up liquid. Saw the squeejee thing and started cleaning the floor, I wanted to sluice it. And all the empty ginger bottles, I stuffed them into another polybag. Absolutely no bother, I was well away. I was laughing to myself. Christ almighty man I knew it for sure, she was coming back, I knew she was coming back, maybe even that selfsame fucking afternoon, I knew it, I knew it for sure. Maybe she would even bring me a present. Christ, yeh, crazy, crazy

Oh my darling

And the sun was shining! Out from between the mighty clouds! Just for that one fraction, the sun it shone from a great height. It seemed clear that this height was great. It was not something ye should have taken for granted at the outset.

And even then, so they say, about the sun.

Yet it wasnay cold. It wasnay even cool. So there was a sense of warmth somewhere. The coolness might have seemed like what ye find in mathematics but mathematics isnay to blame and even that, if we accepted that, it's just an imposition from us. It is too obvious, far too obvious.

But just the thought of what was to come and how it had been, and of how it remains, as it is, at this moment, this ever existing moment.

Cause yet we continue. All of our lives. That is what we do, we continue. We really have to keep on being alert to this fact, because this is what it is, an actual fact.

It makes yer head go.

And so the thought gets forced off into the nothing, into the big blank. Because at the same time there is the coldness, the chill, it is still there, it doesnay go away because ye demand it, ye might want to demand it. But come on!

Plus it was always so bloody hard to speak, even to somebody ye knew really well.

At any time but, how do we do it! we just cannay.

Jill had stopped walking; she was looking at me. I had stopped walking before her. I walked a couple of paces to

be at her side and we carried on side by side. See that
bus? I said, pointing my arm after it. It's an advertisement
for cheese, that's what it is, some sort of advertisement, for
cheese. Amazing innit. The stupidity.

She smiled, uncertain, moved in closer to me, shifting her
bag into her other hand so I could take her arm. It was good
taking her arm. I go about doing things but I always know
how close we are, how close I am. I might want to start afresh
as in a new beginning. However

But I feel this is also a part of it and that it is an indispensable
and crucial – so crucial, so damn crucial, so damn damn
bloody crucial

When I was a boy I was a hell of a blether: a hell of a blether.
I was known for it. I still am a blether to some extent. But
nothing to the likes of how I was. And whatever there is left,
it mostly takes place inside my skull. Unless I'm with her, my
best friend, my wife, lover and partner in this crazy world. If
I'm with her I open out.

There was a couple of people putting out leaflets at the
corner of the lane. With us stopping walking one of them
had stepped over to pass us one. A political meeting of some
kind. Jill was rubbing at the heel of her foot and giving me
dirty looks. Sorry, I said, because I had kicked her.

Did ye even know ye done it?

Naw, honest, I didnay even notice, sorry.

I find that hard to believe, she said and sighed, she took a
leaflet, glanced over it, the person dishing them out seeing
that she did so.

That was what he was doing, the fucking cheek of him.
Such naivety! Unbelievable. I gave him a mean look; he was
puzzled by it. I would have fucking puzzled him one, right
on the chin. Having said that he was a boy, either I would
sink him in one blow or he would weather it and give me

73

a right tanking. Fighting is about fitness. That was my old man's patter. But he knew the boxing, he fucking loved the boxing.

Jill was putting the leaflet into her handbag in such a way I could tell she was worried maybe I was gony give her a showing up by making some sarcastic comment but my head was too full and I just thingwi I stuck my leaflet away into my trouser pocket I suppose who knows, who the hell knows – I dont remember ever seeing the fucking thing ever again, from that minute to this, which is the same thing.

Ye see people's lives; I see them around me; friends, family; the events that went sour. I cannay change these outcomes. I cannay change them. I spoke this to myself through clenched teeth but Jill heard me. It's the idea of the political meeting, I said, can ye imagine it!

Imagine what?

Just the idea of handing out leaflets on the street for something like that! Incredible! Fucking unbelievable. Young people getting conned left right and centre; these bastards, fucking bastards

What . . . ?

But she wasnay listening so I blabbed on about something else altogether, just for something to do, aware of the shoppers and the strollers, wondering if any one of them even knew of my existence. Probably there was at least one. One person was walking this street who either had met me once upon a time or else had a relation or friend that had. You could actually broaden it out to the whole country and say that in Scotland we all know each other, if not we have mutual acquaintances, at the very least. And it has got nothing to do with being a small country; fucking anywhere, anywhere at all – even a country like China. Though there again China is made up of a lot of different areas, provinces, isolated from each other, strangers are a total novelty, viewed with suspicion sometimes, other times treated like royalty, bringing news of the outside world, major events and calamitous happenings, floods and famine, scourges. This is how come their dynasties lasted such a long time, that insularity, a lack of communication, a veritable wealth of that lack. People write about it.

But nah, not even Scotland, it's all different too, like when ye pass through these wee villages down at the border and ye see folk standing outside the door of a newsagent shop, scanning the front page of the paper. It looks like ye must know a couple of the guys, at least a couple, but ye dont know any of them; they have no idea who ye are, no idea of anything about ye, where ye come from, the people ye come from; no really interested, how can they be if they know nothing, if they dont know ye're alive then that's that, too busy with their own wee worries – no that these worries are necessarily 'wee', cause we're talking about their actual lives, wishing they could get new ones, a different outcome to what they're going through, alter the inevitable. Please change my life! Sometimes I can hear them whispering this. Let my fate have a different outcome. Oh please. Please. They dont even know they are doing it, it's a prayer from the depth of their being, dredged out from their subconscious, entirely nonreflective.

It is no place of mine to change these outcomes. I accept that. Sometimes I wish other people would too. But they dont, no without a struggle; on they go persisting and persisting. I dont want to change them. I'm happy the way people are. As far as I'm concerned they should remain exactly as they are. I'm happy with people. Whereas, I wouldnay be happy with gods. One god, two gods or three gods. Who needs them? If people do want to change their lives then it is their responsibility and no mine, nor is it anybody else's, it's theirs; theirs and theirs alone. But they should be happy, content, just to be living instead of not yet entering into the slipstream.

I have seldom felt so damn happy, and content. Then of course Jill! What a woman.

She was looking into the window of a secondhand shop, kidding on she still hadnay arrived at a decision; as if there was any chance she wouldnay enter the shop! Come here, I said and I put my arms round her but she shrugged these arms of mine off – I had a vision of them landing on the street, the beginnings of a Chic Murray joke. Public shows of affection really appal her; she reckons said behaviour is always contrived. She is definitely wrong there but at the same time I know what she means. When we first met I was always grabbing her and she fucking hated it but I didnay cotton on that she was serious, I thought she was sort of

I'm no sure what I thought, except I was wrong. I used to tell her I loved her. The usual outcome to that was silence for the rest of the meal, usually it happened when we were in a restaurant, like that situation where there's a loud babble of voices and ye have to speak loudly to be heard by yer companion and the moment ye choose to bawl the babble stops and there ye are left screaming some secret of yer heart. I was a romantic wee soul. Men are more romantic than women of course that goes without saying, it starts off with the lassies but that soon diminishes: roundabout the same time as a boy stops playing football morning, noon and night and double time on Sundays. In those early days I embarrassed her. I still do. I cannay help it. She thinks it's intentional! In a way it isnay really my fault, it's just how I am, a demonstrative person, a most untypical Scottish male. Or so we're told. Such is what we're always told, that we're an undemonstrative set of buggars, whether ye believe it or not is another story. I'm not generalising from myself, the guys I know are all demonstrative, or at least pretend to be.

What a woman but ye were entitled to grab her. I was, being her man, I was entitled to grab her, it went with the piece of paper. She was entitled to grab me! She never did though. That's a cliché about men and women, the men chase the women all over the place and they never get chased back. Poor old men, ye feel sorry for them. But this after all is nature, it's the natural order.

You still deciding? I said. I pushed open the door, removing said decision from her altogether. I held it open for her. Honest, I said, I'm fine, I'll have a look at the books and records, I feel like browsing. I sang in a whisper: *I'm in a browsing mood*, changing the lyric from the old Ska number, who was it, The Ethiopians? *I'm in a dancing moood.* Oh baby. That great sax.

She half smiled, I'll no be long, dont do anything silly.

What like?

She didnay answer. If she had she would have allowed the possibility. Ye have to hand it to other people, how they get inside yer head. I watched her disappear between a rack of dresses and skirts, in mingling with other women. She was trying to avoid thinking about things. A cousin had phoned her about her auntie earlier in the morning and it wasnay good news. Her auntie was more like a cousin, in fact more like a big sister. Jill's head was full of it and she hadnay reached the stage of talking it over with me. It was still a secret. Her auntie didnt want other folk knowing, especially family. I could deduce from this that it was not terrible. It might have been terrible. But not earth-shattering. Domestic in other words; not a full-blown tragedy. I would find out soon enough. Jill always mulled things over but the final part of this mulling over encompassed the presence of me myself, I, seein wur sels as ithers see us. Sometimes ye dont know what people mean when they tell ye a secret, if ye're married, do they expect ye not to tell yer partner? Maybe they take that into account. If I told a married man a secret it wouldnay surprise me that he told his wife. So much so that I would expect it. If I didnay want the wife to know then I wouldnay tell the guy she was married to, even if he was a close mate, my closest mate. And it wouldnay matter how many hours he spent telling me how confidential he was gony keep it cross my heart and hope to die, god strike me down, that it would be kept strictly confidential; he wouldnay tell anybody, not a soul, except her, his missis. That's what happens with other guys, they know I'm a good listener and can keep a secret, so they tell me them, but I usually wind up telling Jill. Because I take such secrets seriously, I take them in the spirit they're given me. If they werenay truly serious then these guys wouldnay be making an issue about how secretive they were. But it is that very fact, their seriousness, that means I have to give them a good think; and a 'good think' means getting somebody else's opinion. How do people tell ye secrets if not to get ye to make some sort of judgment, they're wanting to hear yer opinion before they make up their mind. The whole thing's crazy, complicated as fuck. Most of my mates are blabbers. I tell them nothing unless the world can hear about it.

There is nothing I could do about her auntie anyway. The only thing I knew was that she couldnay vanish out the problem, whatever it was, and to be honest, I was picking up bits and pieces, it concerned her private life and I mean by that her auntie's man, Jill's uncle properly speaking – a dour chap but honest as the day is long.

All we can do is carry on going, trusting that we can somehow live our way out of it, that together the individual

path becomes clearer. What do we mean by 'together'?
And 'clearer'? What do we mean by the 'path becoming
clearer'?

I cannay even help myself. I cannay even walk down the
street without stepping on her toe, her heel. Amazing.

So, anyway, this part of town we were in, it had a lot of
interesting shopping and things that appeal to Jill and didnay
not appeal to me although it always seemed to her like I made
a big song and dance out of it, like she had to drag me there
kicking and screaming. Even though it was joky, the way I
did it. But browsing through old records and books usually
got me inveigled. She knew me well enough. Mind you it
isnay as if I had a choice in the matter. If there werenay any
books and old records then there would be nothing to look
at at all. Except secondhand tools. That's something I can
spend quarter an hour browsing through. Ye never ever
know what ye'll find, auld spanners are good because it's
hard to get good new yins unless ye buy a whole boxful,
when all ye need's one for some tricky wee job. What a
con, the entire tool manufacturing business, run on the same
principle as the defence industry, get the fucking idiots to buy
the stuff even though they'll lie in some deserted space for the
rest of eternity, kingdom come.

So I'm not exactly a hopeless case, when it comes to
the Saturday morning shopping deal. Except that in saying
this it usually means Saturday afternoon, because either we
get out late or it always drags on and on and by the
time ye get hame it's nearly four o'clock. If she would
just tell me it was Saturday afternoon shopping then all
would be solved, I could make my plans accordingly, I
could do my own bits and pieces in the morning and
save worry. I'm talking about oddjobs about the house.
I like to do them on Saturday afternoons with the radio

blasting, or else I shove on some music if there isnay any fitba.

It was another thing that irked her, me and this need I have to get things organised if not ordered.

This is how she hated me saying I would go with her on these Saturday shopping expeditions. What I couldnt get her to see is that I didnt mind, I didnt mind, not one solitary iota. If there was anything lurking under the surface it was her put it there, she drew inferences where none was intended. So if it was an ordeal getting me places it was only herself to blame. Right enough there had to be some little thing in me because ordeals are ordeals. Something lurked somewhere, forcing her into that defensive mode, that preemptive sort of behaviour she aye got herself into, all tangled up and wanting to scream although she didnay, at least no in public, no as a rule. It had happened once or twice but only at me. In the house. But that is another story altogether. But what doesnt happen in the privacy of one's own home! At least she wasnay a plate tosser. Talking about aunties an auld one of mine was a plate tosser. My dad telt me stories about how when he was visiting her and his brother-in-law he had to keep on ducking, missiles flying everywhere, it was like being a Martian with all these satellites hurtling about in outer space, meteorites.

Never mind.

This charity shop was damn near fucking packed to the gills. An assortment of interesting if not fascinating bodies. But the crowds thinned out by the time one reached the back of the shop where the books were. Plus these three big cardboard boxes falling apart from the sheer weight of records; albums and old 78s all higgledy piggledy in the same stacks and piles. It made me grue to see it. The actual cardboard was split open. The corrugated bit in the middle showed clean through, underwear at the scene of an accident, feelings of hopeless guilt, the person being badly injured. Guilt is the wrong word. It was nothing to do with guilt. More like being put in yer place. It reminds ye how fragile we all are. One gets this tremendous camaraderie.

If I looked at these boxes of records too long my head would go haywire. And the idea of browsing through them, scattering moths and dandelions; selections from The Lower Entwhistle Brass Band Songbook, His Master's Voice, it summed up the british class system right enough, even their damn record labels gave the entire game away.

The shelves up above; a couple of books with unusual covers. Science. But boring, methodological, laden with diagrams and graphs and all manner of alchemically unsound recipes for life-channelling potions only now being discovered from the time of the earlier lost Empire of the Hittites, before even Hammurabi the Lawgiver. These damn books on this shelf were the very books that had been passed down to me from the darkest shrouds of ancient times. I flipped through the introductions, one of which was by an excited person, it made me smile, a recollection of youth. We're all excited at some time in our life, usually at the earlier stages of adulthood. Maybe I would buy them just to annoy this pest of a guy that kept on interrupting me. One of these professional looking tubes, bald nappers and heavy beards, plus brightly coloured braces, fancy waistcoat, funny-styled denim shirt, but fashionable, oh so fashionable. I knew I had seen such shirts recently, probably on the telly. A chubby face with pronounced, red-veined cheeks, giving the appearance of a fervent chap who liked a pint, if ye disregarded his eyes. This pest of a guy was peering along the bottom shelf, making sure he was in before me, sifting through a stack of pamphlets, looking for treasures, lost manuscripts he could flog to the university library, eke out his fifty grand a year.

For a moment he balanced himself by placing his hand on the floor and I thought of crunching down on his fingers with my size nines. Or else giving him a nudge with my knee accidentally on purpose so he would keel over. A rude bastard. If he thought I was moving out his way he was in for a rude awakening. Then I thought of Jill. I couldnay see her but I knew she was watching me. It was for this exact moment she had been in preparation, ever since leaving the house. Aw before that. It spoiled her breakfast.

She would never speak to me again, not for as long as the two of us both shall live.

But that doesnay mean ye've got to put up with shite. Excuse me, I said, and made use of my space, bent down to get into the records even though I knew it would cause me great angst. He gave me a pretend-puzzled look over the top of his specs; he was wanting to know how far he could go. Folk like this are on the look-out for inferior beings, that includes – most of all – people who arenay rude bastards. I didnay even want to look into the records, Top of the Pops compilations from the early 70s, that's all we need.

Lo and behold her apparition. Jill was beckoning me to come hither. I eased myself up from my knees. Aye, I said, only just audible, so the rude bastard could hear me and take what he might, in respect of my disruption of any potential interchange we may or may not have had, consequent upon our encroachments on the other's space. Jill said, That's me. I've been trying to catch your attention for ages.

Dont worry, I said, I wouldnay let a mug like that get to me. When we came out the shop I took a bag from her. Good, I said, what did ye get? I opened the bag for a peek: Clothes?

Yeh.

Great.

I need a coffee, there's a place down the lane.

Sometimes I think you only go shopping to gie yerself an excuse for a coffee and a creamcake.

Give us peace.

I was only kidding Jill christ . . .

The two children with the leaflets were still at the corner, they tried to dish them back out to us again. Jill told them she had one already and they nodded, one of them smiled and looked away. Here it is, I said, sticking my hand in my pocket like I was gony snatch it out. D'ye want it back ya fucking eedjit?

Jill gave me a glare. I followed her. So-called activists, I said, nay wonder! That way some of them have of assuming ye've nay thoughts of any kind, nayn worth a fucking monkey's fucking – jesus christ it makes ye angry

Who cares, she said.

Naw I know.

Who cares?

It just makes ye angry, they dont know what struggle is.

Calm down. She sniffed slightly. Find any books?

There wasnay any books to find.

D'ye want to go home?

Not at all.

Cause I'm no gony go in and sit in that cafe if you're in a mood.

I'm no in a mood.

Cause I would rather just go home.

I'm no in a mood Jill, come on; I'm looking forward to a coffee.

She took a deep breath, and we walked on. The cafe was only another few yards. It was in what used to be a stable or a courtyard or something. What is known as a trendy little damn bistro. The menu was in a side window. The prices werenay too extortionate. Not if you were privvy to the exacerbations of certain jiggerey pokery, the kind that will obtain in these kinds of damn little places.

Still and all, it wasnay cheap. Jill looked at me and entered, I followed. Bastions of unfreedom. The kind of places where people see people and people get seen by people. She was as uncomfortable as me. Uncomfortable is the wrong word. Ye were supposed to be uncomfortable. Ye knew that before ye went in. So ye wind up irritated because of that, because ye cannay find the right word. Maybe there isnay a word. They dont even have a fucking word for it. In other cultures they would have. There would be umpteen words, just for that very experience. I smiled at Jill but she didnay accept it as a smile. It's no that expensive, I said, I dont know why I worry about it.

Ye worry about it because ye're prejudiced.

I am prejudiced; damn right I am, I'm bloody prejudiced, aye, I admit it, I admit it wholeheartedly.

Although ye know it spoils things.

Yeh, it cannay be helped.

Although ye know it's part of us coming out together.

Yeh, yeh I know that, I know.

But ye cant stop yerself.

It appears to be the case, yeh, I cant seem to stop myself. Just like you cannay stop yerself making comments about me looking at the sun.

A waitress appeared; I tried to catch her attention; needless to say I failed. Her head was down, not allowing her attention to be attracted by anybody; so nothing to take personally. Obviously she wasnay the owner. She would be a student. Her body was sticking out the clothes she was wearing. What else do bodies do? Well some of them can sometimes hide, they can so to speak vanish, but this lassie's body was not able to do that, to vanish.

When did I ever make comments about ye looking at the sun?

Can one smoke in here?

How do I know? she said, meanwhile looking around for signs; she pointed to the ashtray on the table. I picked up the menu with an exaggerated flourish. The waitress couldnay have not noticed.

Jill was still speaking. It's bad for yer eyes to look too long at the sun, the glare's too strong. When I nodded she said, Human eyes arenay made for it.

Okay, I replied, but d'ye know any animals that are made for it? None, there isnay any. So I mean what is it ye're saying?

Bats are made for it.

For staring at the sun?

The opposite.

Jill what are ye actually saying?

Listen I just told ye what I said so there's no point in you trying tell me what I'm really saying, as if I'm not even capable of saying what I want to say.

The waitress was standing there. I asked for a coffee and a donut and Jill asked for whatever she asked for, the same as me I think. I tried to use this as an excuse to smile but she had withdrawn from me. The coffees came in a matter of moments. Jill footered with the teaspoon, she gazed about at the different people. Right behind us there were two men and two women, all in their late twenties/early thirties. Maybe not. Maybe the women were in their early twenties. They were attractive looking. One of them had a very rich laugh, but I liked it, she was even I think beautiful although 'beautiful' is the wrong word. It being the West End I figured

her for the BBC or else the theatre business. And here she
was, in the company of do-nothings. I excluded the other
lassie from this, it was the two guys, their very presence, it
seemed to damn near strangle me. Even before I could say
something Jill was on top of it, on top of me. See what I
mean, she whispered, that's exactly what I'm talking about;
ye're so bloody prejudiced. Because of how people look ye've
pigeon-holed them. Ye dont even give them a chance.

What are ye a mind-reader? I didnay actually say a word.

I know ye didnay, ye didnay need to.

Ye're wrong.

I'm not wrong; ye dont give people a chance.

Look, I said, if somebody's wearing an expensive suit then
it doesnay take Sherlock Holmes to work out he's worth a few
quid, or else got some sort of fiddle going somewhere, stuff for
cost price, tax deductible, whatever – even what they buy in
here, it'll be down to the expense account. Ye can tell by their
voices. Listen to them – ye could be standing round in the
main road and ye'd still hear them. They'll have ransacked the
secondhand shop and flogged the damn lot down the Barras
and earned themselves a damn near fortune, before we've
had our bloody breakfast into the bargain, that's what I'm
talking about, it makes ye sick so it does money, money goes
to money, daddy and mummy have got it and they pass it on,
it's genetic; bourgeois bastards.

Ye're mean-minded.

Mean-minded?

That's what ye are, now look at the menu.

That was a good one, mean-minded; if she had wanted to
reduce me to silence. The thing that got me was it was so
spacious. Ye could get a game of football gon in here, I said.
It's vast but eh? Vast!

She ignored me.

Look Jill, all I was saying was how it is for people in a place like this where ye wind up intimidated. The class war continues, know what I mean. Even just the surroundings, it's like they're designed to intimidate ye. If ye let them.

I'm no going to a pub. I just dont want that atmosphere.

I never said nothing about going to a pub.

Well I'm just saying I'm no going to one. She lifted her cup and sipped.

I was only meaning about how if ye're an ordinary person, in a place like this, how ye've got to fight not to be intimidated; ye come in to relax and then ye wind up it's costing ye money just to feel awkward and out of place, a sore thumb. What a deal. Ye wouldnay credit such things could be. If ye came from another country I mean, that's what I'm talking about, from somewhere in Africa maybe, ye would think ye had landed on the moon.

I dont feel awkward, I dont feel out of place, I dont feel anything like that. Anyway, it's licensed.

I know it's licensed.

Ye could have a beer.

Of course I could have a beer, I could have a whisky or a brandy, a glass of wine – you could have a glass of wine, you could have a wee glass of strong red wine. Or else a big glass of strong red wine, take yer pick.

Sometimes ye're stupid do ye know, ye make life so difficult for yerself.

Tell me about yer auntie?

Another time . . .

Jill glanced away towards the counter and the wee kitchen where ye could see a washer-up. I watched the side of her face, the lines; sometimes I liked to draw her, her profile; and her hands, her fingers were oh so different from the likes of mine, I liked to draw them too, and her shoes! her shoes were just so damn neat, her whole body, everything about her. She glanced back and saw I was looking, and she waited for me to speak. I said: It's just I dont want to keep talking. I get sick of talking. I get sick of talking here, in a place like this, just actually talking about life, yours or mine; it makes me feel like a traitor, like I'm gossiping in front of them, like it puts me on a par with them.

I wonder what's happened to the donuts.

Yeh, the donuts. In a strange way that just about sums it up, what's happened to the donuts.

It might sum it up for you but no for me, exclude me from that. I dont have your stupid bitterness.

She said this in the most matter-of-fact way imaginable. Nevertheless, it struck me dumb. I studied the kitchen for a sign of movement. Nothing there either. A Gary Cooper situation, auld Gary Cooper.

What? she said but she was bending down to look inside one of her bags and her head bumped the edge of the table. I moved my hand towards her but she drew me one hell of a look. It's not gony happen again, she said, that's for bloody sure, just no way. And remember this, it was you asked to come, it wasnay me dragged ye.

Ye didnay drag me.

Ye're such a selfish bastard, that's what ye are, ye're just so bloody selfish.

In some cultures they call it survival, self survival.

Is that so?

Self survival, yeh. Gieing yer partner the benefit of the doubt is another way of putting it; it's probably synonymous. I reached for my cigarettes, my fucking hand was shaking. Yeh, I said, fucking synonymous. I saw one of the suits looking my way. Unless he was looking to the kitchen. Maybe I was just in his direction, his line of vision. Good. Fuck him.

I felt very emotional, I wanted to go to the lavatory, just to get away, I needed to get away. She did as well, I knew that. I waited for her to look at me but she didnay. I could see the tension in her face, the strain showing, she could never hide it, then she did look at me and I managed to hold on, to look back at her, managing it.

Every fucking time

Somebody banged into my side and I turned to see who the hell it was but it was just Jinky reaching past, sticking a few empties on the bar. Aw Jinky, I said, know what I mean! I shook my head. He grinned and danced back, fists raised and weaving them roundabout. He was making that gurgling noise; it sounded like he was laughing. Maybe he was. I managed a smile although there was nothing funny about it, his knuckles were flying about six inches from my chin. I never found the guy easy; never. At one time he did box but that isnay how his brains were scrambled. If I had been daft enough to spar back I would have been there all night. He was like one of they dogs ye start petting, ye wind up feart to stop in case they bring out their fangs, get them too excited and they'll take yer heid aff. I stayed where I was. I had two drinks in front of me; a half pint of heavy and a rum. I didnay have much left. I sipped at the heavy.

I thought I heard Jinky going away but naw, when I turned he was right in front of me still doing the ducking and diving routine, plus calling the shots in that made-up version of the rope-a-dope patter he had. It was fucking total gibberish cause his voice-box was off-beam as well. Only about three people in the world knew what he was talking about and I wasnay one of them. Ye could understand how he annoyed some folk, no just strangers. Even if ye were a regular, a cunt like Jinky didnay know the difference. Ye couldnay hit him either. It would have been taking liberties, then the fact nay cunt really knew how good he was at the boxing game so it was a case of a hiding to nothing. Best just to ignore him, hope he would fuck off. He had his work to do anyway: clearing the empties. That was how he got by. It was a wee job he had made for himself. I couldnay have cared less but it was another thing that rankled with some of the regulars. Whether his brains were scrambled or no, the cunt aye wound up with a drink. Either from behind the bar or else a punter might buy him a pint just to get fucking rid of him. That was the way to do it, make a nuisance of yerself. After he went away I massaged my side. I could still feel the blow from his elbow.

I was in company with two other guys, Donnie and Gus Thompson; they were holding onto their drink as well. I had known them for twenty years. One of them had been speaking but I couldnay take it in. I was trying to but it was beyond me. I was getting that feeling again in my chest. I saw Jinky out the corner of my eye. That bastard's dangerous, I said.

Aye he's a nuisance.

No a nuisance Gus that isnay what he is he's dangerous. I lifted the beer and took another wee sip.

Donnie jerked his thumb after him. Ye're fucking right he's dangerous. Us two were in the other night and there's a guy sitting ower there in the corner, so yer man there, he goes and grabs the gless right out his hand; right out his hand, he fucking grabs it – Glenmorangie the guy's drinking, no kidding ye. The guy goes: Heh you, but Jinky ignores him, goes straight ower to the bar with the gless and the guy's got to jump up and rush after him. Know what I mean, the price of drink nowadays, a single malt! Fucking a nicker's worth getting flushed down the sink! Donnie glanced at his brother: Fucking out of order wint it?

Aye, said Gus. And by the way, that guy ye're talking about, I figured him for plainclothes.

Och was he fuck plainclothes.

The way he looked, there was something about him. I says it to ye at the time, no remember?

Donnie raised his eyebrows: These cunts dont drink malt whisky. Fucking tax-payer, know what I mean!

Aye but that's exactly how they do drink it, cause they dont have to fork out for it, it's us; it's us fucking pays for it. See if it was me? brandy and champagne man I'm no kidding ye. It wouldnay be fucking whisky anyway, that's for sure.

It was malt.

Same fucking difference, whisky's whisky – eh Matt?

I gave a nod then lifted the rum to my mouth, took a tiny sip. Stupid conversation. I looked up at the clock on the gantry. Where the hell was Anne? She should have been here by now. Ping pong. I patted myself on the chest. I caught auld Stevie staring at me. He was standing ower the back. I gave him a wave but I dont think he saw. Maybe he was watching something going on behind my back.

It was gony be one of these nights. It wasnay my temper getting worse it was my patience, I just didnay have the patience any more. The fucking brothers grim. What were they rabbiting on about now? The price of drink in general. What else. Their all-time favourite topic. Some pub in the Calton that used to supply the cheapest glass of Eldee in the entire city. I had heard it all before. A fucking thousand times. A million. Only it used to be a pub down the Garscube Road, or was it Garriochmill Road. Who knows; who gives a fuck. It was this kind of patter drove ye nuts. Plus the fact it aye wound up in the past. That was what it was about, the past. It didnay wind up in the past, that was where it started. When ye saw them ye saw twenty years of yer life. Umpteen stupit conversations that drove ye up the wall; that was what it amounted to. How come I was even in their company? Even standing there! Jesus fucking christ all fucking mighty fucking Anne where the fucking hell was she, before I collapsed with a heart-attack or something I couldnay cope with this it was gony drive me right off my trolley.

It was nearly half seven.

Jinky was heading back in this direction. I cupped my hand round the tumbler. I needed a refill but if I did buy one I would need to do something about the brothers. I only had a fiver and some smash, and that included a drink for Anne. Made ye weep so it did, a fiver. Once upon a time . . . But no these days. Even a tenner was fuck all, no for a night out. I had two options; either I could leave them and go and sit at a table, or else I could fuck off aw the gether. They still had half their pints left so there was no way I was gony last them out. Plus I was thirsty. I could maybe nick down *The Ship* and have one there. Then come back and wait outside the door. Except now she was late I didnay know when she would get here. I might go to another pub then two minutes later in she would come. That was what happened in this life.

The barman was looking my way. He was new. Sometimes the comments he made, they werenay quite sarcastic but ye felt like it was only a hop, step and a jump. They said he was a good fitba player but if he was that good how come he worked behind the bar. Straightforward. Ye had to laugh at some of them. Sometimes I heard him rabbiting on about politics. A load of shite. Still and all but he was young, ye've got the right to be young, the right to make an arse of yerself. That funny kind of hair style he wore. One of my daughters' boyfriends had exactly the same. He was a cheeky wee cunt and all.

Donnie was staring into my face. I'm talking about a gless,

he said, I mean you know that yerself Matt you used to drink in the fucking place.

Right, I said, aye.

Sometimes ye felt like dropping deid, just to escape the company. It wouldnay have mattered. Naybody would have noticed. These two bastards would just have carried on talking, whether ye drapped deid or no, it just wouldnay matter, they would fucking step ower ye, or else carry on talking; they would carry on talking to ye, meanwhile the ghost out yer body's rising up, and they're still fucking talking – gie us a break ya cunt I'm trying to join the spirit world!

I fingered the glass of rum; this wouldnay last long either, two more fucking sips. Ping pong. One of these weird movies where ye see cunts' heids swimming in and out of focus. That was what like it was. Donnie was staring right at me again. Or at somebody ower my shoulder. Maybe my ghost was out my body already. Or else some other poor cunt. A bit of peace; that was what I needed, a bit of peace and fucking fuck knows what, just peace; peace.

Alright?

What?

The way ye're holding yer chest, what is it heartburn?

Aye, I said, it's a pint of milk I need.

Ye've got to watch it Matt, the auld health and that.

Aye right, aye.

The black rum isnay the best of drinks.

If I want a packet of zantac I'll go to the chemist Gus know what I mean, I'm just having a wee drink, okay, I'm passing the time, that's what I'm doing, I'm passing the time. I lifted the rum and swallowed it, swallowed the lot. That left the beer.

I couldnay even buy myself a drink, if I put my hand in my pocket I was fucked; one round and that was me. In the

auld days I could have went round the backcourts and sang a
song, held out the bunnet and aw that, pennies from heaven,
the women would have threw me down a few bob. With
my luck it would have been a piece on fucking jam.

It was my ayn fault for coming in here; I should have telt
Anne someplace else. Convenience is all it was. If I wanted
to be anonymous, if I didnay want to see nay cunt, what
the fuck was I doing here? If it was a nightmare it was only
myself to blame. Nay excuses. And it wasnay the brothers'
fault, poor bastards. But that was the amazing thing about it,
half a lifetime. Incredible.

Donnie was talking to me: I was saying there about Tam
Delaney Matt ye seen him recently?

Is he no still in the bakery?

Aye but ye seen him recently? The cunt's eating his ayn
cakes, he's ballooned to fuck man right out. Telling ye, fat
as fuck, ye want to see his neck – he's no fucking got one!
He cannay stop eating.

Maybe he's fucking hungry, I said, I know the feeling.

The two of them laughed. I did too, spluttering ower my
beer. The barman stared at me; he was pouring a pint of
guinness for some lucky bastard. Gus was wiping his mouth
with the cuff of his sleeve. I saw water in his eyes, trying
no to laugh again. He was one of these guys that cannay
stop once they start; all ye had to do was look at him.
Now he sniffed, turning his head away, getting himself
the gether.

Aye, said Donnie, he's driving a new cavalier.

I nodded, reached for a jug of water and poured a drop
into the empty rum tumbler, swirled it about. No like when
he had that auld morris, I said, mind that yin?

Never fucking went anywhere. The cunt spent half his
life underneath the bastarn thing. Now he couldnay get

95

underneath it! One of they sumo wrestlers Matt ye want to see the girth!

He's happy but eh?

Oh aye he's happy, nothing against the guy.

I shrugged and lifted the tumbler, sipped at the water, my hand round the half pint glass. Donnie was reaching for his pint and I saw him giving a quick look to Gus. Naw, I said, just how some guys put it on and that the weight know, if ye're driving a delivery van all day, plus the fact if ye like a pint, ye cannay help it, the big belly and aw that, ye're bound to get a gut.

Aye well fair enough, said Gus, he aye liked his bevy; it's no something ye're gony hold against him.

I aye liked Tam; good big guy.

Auld Stevie appeared. He must have been playing the puggy machine, or else away for a pish. He tapped me on the shoulder: What've you chucked the doms?

Naw, I'm just no playing the night.

Ye didnay play a fortnight ago either.

Stevie I'm just taking a wee rest; it's allowed innit?

Aw aye it's allowed, aye ... He sniffed, his forehead wrinkling. He was one of these auld guys that keep getting bees in their bunnet. One of his traits was to ask about yer wife and the way he did it made it seem like in his opinion ye were neglecting her. That was what he did now, just as he was about to leave: So where's Anne the night? he said, giving me a look.

I telt him I didnay know. I could have said more but no in front of the brothers. No in front of him either when it comes down to it. It was always amazing to me how people expected ye to dish out personal information. Maybe she's in the house, I said.

Ah well, it's a cauld night ... He sniffed again, stood

for another wee minute. He didnay like the brothers and was avoiding looking at them. Naybody liked them very much, no really. I could put up with them. Mind you I just didnay have the same option, I knew them too long, it made it difficult being anti-social. It took too much energy. I couldnay be fucking bothered; it was either them or some other cunt, that was the way I looked at it.

It did dawn on me but about auld Stevie; he was trying to find out if I was skint, if that was how I hadnay signed in for the match. In some ways it was right but in other ways it had fuck all to do with it. If I had had a few quid I still wouldnay have been playing. Plus anyway I was meeting Anne. She's due any minute, I said.

He looked at me, puzzled.

I'm supposed to be meeting her. I looked up at the clock.

Aye, nay bother Matt. He passed on to the far side of the bar where the tables were set up. I saw him join with another couple of guys from the squad, then he peered back at me.

What is there a match on the night? said Gus.

Aye.

Who they playing?

Couldnay tell ye.

Obviously I knew who they were playing but I didnay feel like passing on the information. It would have meant the conversation going on longer. No just that. Something else too. But I couldnay be bothered working out what it was. I took another look at the clock: She should've been here by now.

Women eh!

Aye that's right Gus women. I smiled but turned away. It made ye laugh. Neither of them knew fuck all about women, they had lived with their maw since the day they were born.

I've no seen Anne for a while either, said Donnie, how's she keeping?

She's keeping fine aye keeping fine.

Still got the wee job?

Aye.

She wasnay feeling that hot before but wint she no?

That's right . . . I fingered the half pint tumbler; the two of them were looking at me, waiting for me. Just a stage, stages ye know we go through stages, I said, we all go through stages.

What is she no keeping that good?

I've just telt ye she's fine Gus christ almighty.

Donnie gave Gus a look that he meant me to clock, so I would know it wasnay something he would have said. I couldnay be bothered with all this kind of stuff it was too tiring, all the subtleties, how to behave in company in one easy lesson. The trouble was the one easy lesson lasted a lifetime, that was how long it took ye to fucking get it, to grasp it; by the time ye did grasp it ye were fucking deid.

Where is it she comes frae again?

The southside.

Govan?

Naw, no Govan, naw. I lifted the half pint glass.

Heh, I was hearing about Smiddy's funeral, some kind of schemozzle.

It was blown out of proportion, I said.

Was it no to do with his neighbours?

Drink was talking, I know who telt ye.

Aye right, right. Mind you but auld Smiddy, he could fair batter the bevy.

Jesus christ he wasnay even fifty. Auld Smiddy! he wasnay even fucking fifty!

He had aged but Matt come on.

We've all aged.

Aye but fuck sake . . . !

Donnie the guy had problems: a fucking heart condition.
Aw I know, I know, he wasnay well, I know that.
He hadnay been well for a while.
I know that.
Christ sake.
Get Jean to gie ye a sandwich, said Gus.
What?
Get Jean to gie ye a sandwich.
Ping pong. I looked to where he was pointing. Three big plates of sandwiches sitting on the other side of the bar; cornbeef and gammon or something, cheese. Jean would have gave me a sandwich. I didnay feel like one but, if I had I would, I would have asked. They would be dished out eftir the game. They were for the players, the hospitality. If the boys won the night they would go third top of the league so it was quite important. No that I felt guilty. There were other players as good as me anyway, better. And all these commitments, they drive ye fucking bonkers.

I get a touch of it myself, said Gus, but I find if I eat now and again it puts it right. Even a dry biscuit, with a wee tait milk. Guinness is good too, I'm talking about indigestion, it's the creaminess.

Guinness is good for you.
The auld advert eh I mind it well, the penguins!
Pelicans.
Fucking penguins.
Them were the days.
Matt you're forty-four int ye? Cause I mind ye were way above us at school. Were you no in fourth year when I started?

That's right, said Gus, I was in second and Matt was in fourth.

Well I mind I was in fucking fourth year aye but I dont mind fuck all else.

Oh aye Matt I was in second and Donnie was in first. Course ye aye know the big boys but they never know you, no if ye're younger.

That's a fact.

At school especially because there's that many folk. I mean see when we were at school, how many did they have to a classroom? Know what I mean, nowadays, they dont know they're living.

Fucking better believe it, said Donnie.

And now here we were back to schooldays; prattling on about this and that, then one of them was talking about the jannie – Mister Small. Mister Small, I remembered him clear as a bell. How could ye forget him. He had one of these wee moustaches like David Niven; strolled about the place with his thumbs in his waistcoat pockets. Sometimes he gave ye a wink if he caught ye looking at him. Hardly ever spoke. Gallus as fuck but I liked him. Most of the boys did. He was tough but he was fair, didnay say much, didnay have to. I could even remember the house he lived in, right by the playground gate. When his wife was hanging up the washing ye saw inside the door. It looked great. Heh, I said, d'ye mind that house he lived in?

Ye kidding! said Donnie.

Gus was chuckling. I used to like carrying messages just so's I could see inside the lobby. Know what I mean, when ye're a boy, ye're aye curious, ye're wanting to know what's going on. See upstairs and downstair houses! I used to fucking love them so I did!

Ye still do, said Donnie. Nay kidding ye Matt see whenever he goes into one!

Mind you, it was more like a fucking palace wint it!

100

Massive, I said, fucking massive; ye could see the kitchen through the back, they had two cats and one great big fucking huge dog.

A husky.

A husky?

A fucking husky, aye.

Ye sure about that? I looked at Gus who gave a slight shrug of the shoulders.

Honest, said Donnie, that was what it was a fucking husky, gen up, the first yin I ever saw outside the movies. That's how I remember. It looked ferocious but it wasnay. Ye could clap it.

I wouldnay have fucking clapped it.

Ye could've but Matt that's what I'm saying.

Was he no an armyman? asked Gus.

I think so, said Donnie.

Och there's nay fucking danger about that, I said, he was an armyman from way back. Strict as fuck, but fair; aye fair. Christ.

A name like that tae Mister Small!

Mister hard-as-fuck would've been better.

Aye, I said, mind that time he broke up the fight with Willie Peterson and Big Simmie? Round the back of the playground with that mental teacher? No mind? Fuck sake what a fight that was! Mister Small walking in; christ almighty, remember!

Cannay say I do, naw . . . Donnie had his pint to his mouth.

Aw fuck, it was a famous yin! The mental teacher. Willie was gony fucking have him and all. You must have heard about that one?

I'm no sure if I have.

It was a famous yin.

It was maybe before our time. Big Simmie was involved?

Him and Willie Peterson. Ye mind Willie Peterson?

Eh . . .

No mind him?

Dont think so.

Christ.

I was gony say more but didnay bother. It was hard to believe they had never heard about this fight. There was naybody in that school hadnay heard about it. It was just too big.

That was how ye could never quite trust the brothers, ye never knew what they were thinking. Ye could be talking and ye would see them gieing wee looks to one another. It isnay like they were taking the piss. Just something. Who knows.

The conversation stayed with boxing. The pair of them were into it and went to a few shows; they followed the amateurs. It was one of their big things. Bobby Reid's name cropped up. It wasnay so much I knew him but I knew of him. Aye fine, I said, if ye're talking about Bobby Reid.

What about him?

Nothing about him, just I knew a couple of guys trained with him.

Aye right Matt but that's what we're talking about, Joe McDonald, he had the height as well, just like Big Simmie, a big long reach.

Mind Joe was fighting the barber? said Gus.

Right, said Donnie, that's what I mean, these big guys, so often they're just no tested. Time and again ye see it. And ye knew that with Joe, sure, aye, he might've been big but he wasnay fucking I mean he was skinny as fuck, a bag of bones; there wasnay an ounce of meat on him; ye wouldnay have fucking threw him to a cat neither ye would.

The barber could fight but.

102

I'm no saying he couldnay but once ye got inside Joe's defence christ easy pickings, plus the fact if ye're a wee guy ye'd be using the fucking heid, ye'd be aw ower him, if ye'd any experience at all.

Aye hang on, I said, we're no talking about men we're talking about boys, at least that's what I'm talking about, Simmie and Willie Peterson, a fight in the fucking school playground, there's a fucking difference.

Aw aye.

A fight between boys.

Sure, said Donnie, when he was a boy, Big Simmie could handle himself then, sure, I'm no saying he couldnay.

Bobby Reid was wanting him down the gym I mean come on, he could fight like fuck.

Bobby Reid kept open doors.

No quite.

Any boy that showed promise.

Aye so he was showing promise. That's all I'm saying. You're away off talking about the boxing ring. Joe McDonald . . . Fuck, you're talking about men.

Aye but Joe wasnay that good Matt that's all we're saying.

He went in for the 'Scottish' christ Gus he couldnay have been that fucking bad! Know what I mean! Anyway, it doesnay matter, I was only talking about Simmie and that time with Willie Peterson, when they were boys, when we were at school. I shook my head, lifted the glass of water, fucking conversation, I stared across the bar.

I dont mind of that other guy at all, what was his name again Willie Peterson? he was definitely at our school?

Gus he was in my fucking class, I said, it was a famous fucking fight. I mean jesus christ *I* must have telt ye about it afore, never mind nay other cunt.

Gus shrugged, watching Donnie light another cigarette. I

felt like one myself and I had fucking chucked it ten fucking year ago.

Ping pong jesus christ, I sipped the water.

At least they had shut up. We stood there. Donnie was looking across to the telly like he was interested in whatever it was, Coronation Street.

I had to calm down. My nerves were shot to fuck, how come I dont know, except them, these two cunts.

But I shouldnay have been taking things as bad as this, it was crazy. My fucking belly tae it was havoc down there. A pint of milk, that was what I needed. Or a bowl of soup, I had made a pot earlier on. A big ham-bone off the butcher; he wasnay a bad cunt, I sometimes saw him in the betting shop.

And now for the second time I saw Gus sneaking a look at Donnie and it dawned on me he might be worried – about me, me with my fucking heartburn. It was true but we were all getting auld. Smiddy was a warning christ we were all liable to fall down, at any time.

At least I had weans. That made it easier. Maybe it didnay. Maybe it was better without them, then ye could fucking drap deid any time ye liked, ye could fucking choose it, choose yer spot.

Christ, I sipped the water. I held the tumbler in my hand in case Jinky appeared, which he could do at any moment, he was a fucking ghost, an apparition. I saw a wee crowd round the puggy machine, the young team, probably he was among them. What dough he had went on that. He wasnay alone but, no in this place. No mad gamblers, just mad. Gamblers wouldnay have wasted their time. I heard Donnie say something but I never caught it. I waited a wee minute to get the gist of what they were saying but it was lost and gone forever. When there was a gap in the conversation I said: Right enough, thinking about it, the guy I was telling

104

ye about, Willie Peterson, he was a bit of a dark horse, aulder than the rest of us if I mind right.

Donnie was looking at me.

The guy that gave Big Simmie the bating, I said, he was only at our school a wee while, he came from somewhere else; ower the East Coast I think, Fife or someplace, Willie Peterson.

That was fourth year? said Gus.

Aye, he was in my class. No a bad fitba player by the way, good in the air – one of they Joe Harpers; legs like fucking oak trees. We played the gether a season. He used to play off me. I could hold a ball, he was nippy as fuck. See in the penalty area! Ho. Slide the ball through and that was that; anywhere I mean, inside that box. Fucking born striker. We done well; took a trophy. Them were the days . . . !

The school-team?

Naw Gus the Y.M., it's the Y.M. I'm talking about.

Right.

Willie didnay play for the school. Some reason . . . Cannay mind.

Course no everybody played for the school.

Fucking better believe it.

Naw but he would've walked in Donnie, being honest. Naw, it's funny that right enough. I wonder how the fucking hell . . . I cannay remember; I cannay fucking remember.

Big Simmie played for the school but Matt didnt he?

Aw aye, good player, Big Simmie. See but he couldnay get into the Y.M. side; he couldnay fucking get into it. It pissed him off. Course ye have to remember about the Y.M. it was different age-groups, plus the religion course ye've got to remember that tae, the time I'm talking about, it didnay matter who the fuck ye were, if ye were any good, pape or a blue nose it didnay matter; I'm no saying ye'd make the

line-up but guaranteed ye were in the frame, I'm talking
about if ye were any good. A guy called Jackie Bailey done
the selection. No a bad cunt. The big yin fucking hated him!
He hated me and all if it comes to it!

Who Big Simmie?

Aye!

He hated you?

Aye! Well no fucking hated me exactly; more like – fuck
knows. But see in street games and that when we were playing
the gether, he loved being up against me, he didnay want to be
in the same side, he wanted to be up against me. So he could
kick fuck out me! Or try to!

I thought you and him got on alright.

Aye nowadays! It's still what ye call an uneasy friendship.
The last time I saw him, ower in Clydebank, some boozer,
I got up to go for a pish; nay kidding ye, the cunt took a
fucking swipe at my ankles. When I'm passing the table! I'm
telling ye. He fucking lashed out. Honest to god. Mind you
he still fucking missed. Ya cunt ye I says ye still cannay get
near me.

Was he serious?

The thing about Big Simmie, he was aye a huffy bastard.
He's still a wee bit like that, I've got to say it. I like him ye
know but . . . When I says Willie Peterson was moody, fair
enough, aye, but he wasnay huffy.

I didnay know he was like that.

Oh aye christ Simmie! See we baith played for the school.
That was how he got annoyed, he couldnay see the logic. He
thought he should've walked into the Y.M. side. Then Willie,
Willie was the last straw. He didnay even play for the school!
And he wasnay a tim. If he had been a tim I think Simmie
wouldnay have fucking minded, he would have accepted it.
Now I'm no saying Willie was a better player, being honest,

106

just different, different styles. Simmie was a big lanky cunt as ye know. Mind you but he couldnay outjump Willie, like I'm saying, one of they Joe Harpers, ye couldnay knock him off a ball. And nay nerves, nay fucking nerves; if he had any he kept them in his fucking pocket. A fucking born striker. He would put himself anywhere, brave as fuck, a lion so he was a fucking lion. Simmie was more a knock-down type of guy, wee flick-ons with the heid and aw that. Ye could have used the two of them the gether, but if ye had to choose one it would have been Willie. Fuck sake but see for that one season! Christ. What a squad. A guy called Peter Molloy was with us, he played on the left, mid-field, a defender but he could fucking crack a ball, he scored a good few for us; it was the Boys Guild he should've been playing for, he turned out for the Roch's later on. Peter was a rare player. Telling ye but I mind even afore the league started proper we had a friendly with Possil and we fucking bate them two-one. What a game, Possil, they didnay like getting fucked.

They still dont.

That wee bastard McKenzie was with them, I dont know if ye mind of him, Danny McKenzie, he went south. Good wee player but a fucking dirty little fucking bastard so he was.

Danny McKenzie? said Gus.

Danny McKenzie, aye.

Did he no go junior?

Naw. I laughed, shook my head: Naw, he went down to England straight. Me and him had a few goes but I'll tell ye that. The game I'm talking about, the Possil, I'm no saying we ran rings round them, I'm no meaning that. It was just fucking . . . Ye want to have seen Jackie Bailey eftir the game, I thought he was gony fucking kiss us all! He couldnay talk! he just went about gieing us all cuddles! Ye would have thought we had won the fucking cup!

107

I laughed again then lifted the half pint glass to my mouth and swallowed the beer.

I thought wee Danny went junior.

Naw. Naw he didnay.

Ye sure?

Positive. Straight senior, some English team. There was a few of them went junior but he didnay.

I think I mind Peter Molloy, said Donnie.

Do ye? Good, aye.

Mid-field player ye say?

Aye. Aye he was a rare player Peter so he was; solid as fuck, great passer of a ball. One of these guys ye know, deid balls and that, he could fucking put it anywhere; hell of a powerful shot. Wound up he went to Australia; one of these semi-pro deals where they set ye up with a job. He turned out with the Roch's for a couple of seasons. He looked a cert to make the grade.

McKenzie was good but surely?

Aw aye I'm no saying he wasnay, just he was a dirty wee bastard.

Good man to have in yer team but!

He wasnay in my team Gus he played with the Possil.

Naw I'm no meaning that, just somebody that can stick in the clog, ye need guys like that.

Ah well, sometimes.

Aw come on Matt!

They can fucking cost ye.

Ye talking about infringements?

Uch. I shrugged. I had the empty glass in my hand, I lifted the tumbler, took a wee sip of the water; nay point talking.

The brothers were waiting.

Nay point talking, I said, it's a different game, a different game.

Ah well it's changed, sure.

Beyond all recognition.

No quite.

There's that many cloggers in the game nowadays. They were always there but it just seems worse.

I just nodded; it was a time to drop out the conversation. I couldnay believe I had done so much yapping. Ye would have thought it was the highlight of my life the way I had been telling it. A game of football I played at 15 years of age, nearly thirty year ago. What a joke. The amazing thing was I remembered so much about it. I could even mind wee clumps of grass here and there, the mud through the centre circle. Fucking twilight time right enough. A friendly game and all. Crazy. It was me that was the joke. I saw Donnie half-leaning across the bar, he was flagging a note, trying to catch Jean's attention. Then I heard him asking for a dark rum. I said to Gus: Is he getting me a drink?

Aye.

Right . . .

I went to the toilet. When I came back and looked at the wall-clock I saw it was five to eight. Anne was nearly an hour late. It isnay that she was never late but where she was coming frae it was a bus every half hour; this meant she wouldnay be here for another twenty minutes at least. It was lager the brothers were drinking, I could just about return a round.

Jean was giving me a look.

Awright Jean! I said.

Aye.

Some weather eh!

No half.

She kept looking at me, a smile on her face, I think she expected me to say something else, what I dont know. Donnie laid the drinks in front of me. Cheers Donnie, I said, acting like it was a usual state of affairs. He gave me a nod, stood there waiting while she poured the two pints.

Gus turned his head to whisper: Rare fucking barmaid but int she, ye never have to stand with her.

Aye no like some of them, I said, they should be fucking out there emptying dustbins. See that new young guy that's started? fucking cheeky bastard by the way.

Gus just smiled. He'll grow out it.

I know he'll grow out it, but he's a fucking know-all. See the state of the haircut! I mean what's all that about? When we were wee they called it the bowl!

Yer fucking maw done it or yer grannie, said Donnie.

Aye I know. Nowadays they pay for the fucking privilege. All sorts of dough. They're all wearing it tae, ye see them on the telly, the fucking lot, they've all got it – fucking follow-my-leader. I shook my head, lifting the rum. Cheers Donnie, I said, and took a sip at it.

Nay bother Matt.

Gus was chuckling. Our nephew's got one.

I fucking noticed, said Donnie.

It looks auld fashioned but it isnay, it's modern. I chinned him about it the other week; he just fucking looked at me. Cannay blame him but, us auld bastards!

Aye Gus that's all very well, I said, but ye dont know what they're up to nowadays, that's the fucking problem.

Dope.

Dope and fuck knows what, it's a worry, I'm telling ye.

They had their pints now, the two of them, we stood there. The other end of the bar had got busy; the opposition had arrived. That wee bit of tension. I knew the feeling. The matches would have been getting picked. I saw a couple of guys shaking hands. Jinky was collecting empties and straightening up the domino tables: one of the opposition

110

was trying to talk to him, a wee guy with a big gut, I thought I knew him from somewhere, but that aye happens.

Mind you, he did look familiar.

The rum might have been bad for the digestion system but it done the brains a power of good. It was an auld guy I used to work beside gave me the taste for it. Folk drank it with coke and other stuff but I liked it the way it was; sometimes I had a glass of water at the side, a chaser. Especially if I was drinking in the house. No that I drank in the house very much. Just sometimes if there was people in.

I heard myself doing one of these funny wee breaths. Fucking weird. It was a habit I was getting. I had got it already. Just out the blue it would happen, I could be sitting there watching the telly, reading a book, whatever, and then I would do it; just this wee kind of breath, a sharp yin. It meant my head was somewhere else, without realising it, I was away worrying about something or other. It was a sigh.

I wondered about phoning the house, the daughters wouldnay be there but the boy would, he was always there, he never fucking went anywhere except his room, the room to the bathroom – the room to the bathroom to the fucking kitchen. That was if ye could get him to go to the fucking kitchen cause he never fucking ate, ye couldnay get him to fucking eat. Ye made him a meal, he didnay fucking eat it. Telling ye, I said, nowadays, they dont fucking eat. That young yin of mine, I'm fucking sick cooking him his dinner, the fucking cat gets it. Best fed pet up they flats so it is, fucking mince and mashed potatoes, know what I mean, fish teas it gets. It's no fucking funny.

Naw, said Gus.

Is he still playing the snooker? said Donnie.

Nah.

What is he chucked it?

Fuck knows. I took a long swallow of beer.

He's good but int he? Donnie had brought out his fags while he was talking. I thought he was gony offer me one again but he didnay. He was on his tod as the lone smoker. I felt like taking one just to noise up Gus. It isnay that I liked one brother better than the other, no really, just how Gus got his wee dig in now and again, and smokers are an easy target. Maybe it was their maw's fault. One of these destructive auld bastards; totally selfish the way I read it. The pair of them should have fucked off years ago. Ye have to break out. So what if their maw needed looking after? They could have done it at a distance, they could have fucking took it in turns. Kept their ayn wee flat, one of them could have went one month and the other one the next. Something could have been worked out. Now there was nay escape, they were stuck with each other.

What a nightmare.

I felt the air on my tongue. It was like my nose was permanently blocked, my lips permanently cracked. The council had changed the central heating system and every cunt was going about with dry lips and blocked fucking noses. Unless it was the alcohol. They say it dries ye out. Maybe it was time to go off it again. Even just for a wee while. It was a thing I could do. One time I lasted three months. I didnay find it a problem. In fact I was beginning to think this was how I was having such difficulty going to the pub; I think I was in the process of taking a scunner. That was how it went with me. Things got worse and worse till sooner or later I just wrapped it in. Whatever it was. The same when I chucked the smoking, I didnay work it all out in advance, just one morning I woke up and thought, fuck that for a game. I could do the same with the booze.

Ye were telling us about that fight, said Gus, mind? Mister Small.

Aw aye . . .

There wasnay much to tell but I telt them anyway. I felt a bit sorry for them. Ye heard a couple of the guys talking behind their back. Some of it had to rub off on me. It couldnay help rub off on me because a lot of them was me, their memories, the way they were as boys, the way I was: shared experiences. We could remember the same wee incidents, the same auld folk about the streets, the same wee shops and backcourts, the good dykes for climbing; all that sort of stuff.

It was like we were the same, except we werenay. But sometimes it was a weird thing like they were a pair of vampires. I was aye having to watch myself, that I didnay tell them major secrets – one night I nearly wound up telling them about Doreen, this lassie I used to know. Being honest about it I cannay mind if I did cause I might have, I had had a few pints. But I seem to remember stopping myself. I was aye waiting for her name to crop up in conversation so I could find out how much they knew. Doreen had stayed round the corner from me afore I got hitched, back in the auld place. Me and her sort of went out the gether. Sometimes I still thought about her. Weird. Like a true-love romance or some fucking thing, a woman's magazine. I could go months without ever thinking about her, not once. Other times I just couldnay get rid of her, the thought of her. It went in bouts, the way some guys hit the drink, or the gambling.

I cupped my hands round the tumbler and the half pint glass. Jinky was in the vicinity, I could sense him, and there he was with two piles of empties, baith stacked in a oner, the Tower of Pisa they should have called the cunt.

An inch of beer left and nay rum. I had swallied the fucking

lot just about, I had done it without even realising. I smiled.
I couldnay help smiling. I dont know what about. I think I
was just fucking – I dont know. But the hard fact is I had a
fiver and some smash, and that included a drink for Anne,
and now there was nay option, the brothers had to get their
pint. Never mind.

John MacDonald was heading thisaway. It didnay surprise
me, he was captain of the domino team and took it serious
as fuck. Heh Matt, he said, you playing the night? Cause yer
name isnay down.

Naw John I didnay put it down. Anne's coming in, I'm just
waiting for her, we're going out. Yez no got a team like?

Instead of speaking he sniffed. He got near me and turned
his head so I had to lean close, and when he spoke he spoke so
naybody could hear bar me. Ya cunt ye, he said, ye skint?

Nah.

Ye sure?

Aye.

He still looked at me.

Aye, I said, I'd have had my name down otherwise. I'm
waiting for Anne, she's late.

Ah right Matt nay bother.

We're supposed to be gon somewhere.

By this time what we were saying was ordinary conversation so the brothers judged that to mean it didnay
matter if they heard or no and Gus came in: Hard game
the night John?

They're aw fucking hard Gus know what I mean. John
hadnay looked at him when he spoke and now he walked
back to the domino table.

Poor auld Gus, he was just being friendly. I saw Donnie
give him a wee look and I thought to myself, Donnie, you're
a bitter bastard.

114

Funny that, it hadnay occurred to me afore. Bitter. That was what it was.

Unless maybe he just didnay like Gus. I had a brother and three weans myself so it was a kind of weird thing to think, except it made sense, ye can love yer family but ye dont have to like them. Nothing new about that it's a fucking auld story. I felt like asking them. How come yez go about the gether if yez fucking hate each other? But maybe it was just Donnie hated Gus, and no the other way about.

Jesus christ, even thinking about stuff like that, it summed it all up. And bowl-heid was watching me. Young guys like him were a pain in the neck. Them and their fucking politics. They thought they knew it. Sometimes ye felt like grabbing them, gieing them a shake, the teeth rattling in their fucking heid.

And just leaving them there, no saying fuck all, just giving them a shake and then leaving them. Cause what was there to say? Nothing. Ye could spend yer life talking.

I would buy the brothers a drink and get to fuck. I wouldnay get one for myself, I would just head up the road. Anne would know where I was, if she was coming, maybe she wasnay coming, maybe I had mixed it up.

Ping pong right enough.

Donnie said, Alright Matt?

Aye, just fucking thinking about something. I tapped myself on the chest. Look at the state of this, I said, the fucking leather jacket!

What about it?

She bought me it.

It's alright.

What ye kidding! looks like a plate of cauld fucking porridge! Fucking colour, *Age Concern*, that was where she got it.

Some good bargains in there.

Aye I know but fuck sake I mean even if it was brand new. She took a chance I would like it. It's fucking auld fashioned but int it?

It's alright.

Nah it's fucking . . . it's long out of date, my boy wouldnay be seen deid in it.

For some reason I started laughing, no loud, just fucking quiet, thinking about how she came hame with it and took it out the bag, held it up, a worried look on her face. Telling ye, I said, some fucking turn so she is, know what I mean, comes in with all sorts of stuff. She got us a pair of trousers to go with it; fucking three pair of braces they needed! Ye want to have seen them! I says jesus christ Anne.

Aye but come on Matt women cannay buy men trousers, it's like shirts, they cannay buy them either, they never know what the style is, long collars, short collars, button-downs; they dont fucking know – same with trousers.

Ye cannay get a pair of trousers these days anyway, nayn of them fucking fit, plus they're all wide as fuck.

Aw I know. Heh, d'ye mind about fucking McDougal, Billy McDougal? how he got the yul brynner? mind that yin? he had went baldy at the back and naybody telt him? d'ye mind! And he hadnay seen it himself so what happens, his youngest lassie tells him doesnt she, the horrible truth and aw that, so what does Billy do he turns round and wallops her for being cheeky, then he discovers she's telling the truth, so off he goes and gets it all off – penance! No mind that? Penance, that's what he called it, a fucking baldy!

Ye could understand it but, said Donnie, hitting the wean for nay reason.

Gus was laughing. Aye but that was a good yin, McDougal

and that thinking he'd a fine heid of hair, nay cunt had telt him different.

They were all too feart, I said, the fucking temper that cunt's got!

Daddy ye've got nay hair, ye're baldy. Then getting walloped!

Aye, but Matt's right Gus the same man, he could be a bad bastard, that time back in the street, Guy Fawkes night – mind that? he got wee Katy round the back of the chip shop?

Oh christ aye, I mind that yin – eh Matt?

I smiled and lifted the glass, swallowed the rum.

You were there wint ye?

The brothers were waiting but I just shrugged, I wasnay gony say fuck all. These kind of stories werenay funny. Maybe once upon a time but no now. Wee Katy for christ sake. Who the hell wanted to rake up all that auld stuff? There was a time and a place. Ye telt these stories when ye were a boy, and ye maybe laughed at them, fair enough, but no once ye got aulder. These cunts that still telt stories like that, there was something creepy about it. One thing for fucking certain, ye wouldnay let them near yer fucking weans. I wouldnay have thought the brothers were like that but who knows, ye wondered what they spoke about when they were in the house, just the two of them, sitting there with the bottle of wine and a half dozen cans.

Jinky had spotted my empty tumbler and unlike the barman he didnay give a fuck about the proprieties. I had done in the beer without thinking, I had swallied the lot. I upturned the empty half pint and dunked the last drops into the rum glass: What ye drinking? I said, lager is it? I waved to the barman: Two of lager son!

Fuck sake Matt, said Donnie.

Two of lager ye said . . . ? The barman already had his

117

hand on the tap and the pint glass underneath. So he had heard me the first time. I just looked at him. These daft questions, there's nay need for them.

Ye dont have to bother, said Donnie.

Naw naw christ I just wish I could stay for another myself but I cannay, I better head. Anne's probably sitting up the house waiting for me. Know what I mean, I think I've fucking mixed things up again!

Would she no have phoned but?

What?

She knows where ye'd be, she would just phone here.

It depends. Maybe, aye . . . I shrugged, I think she will be there but. I had the fiver out. The barman took it, watching the beer pour while he hit the till, one of these computer efforts where ye dont have to count fuck all, ye just hit a button.

What if she turns up, said Gus, will we just tell her ye've gone hame?

Aye. Aye do that eh, ta. I got the change and drank the last of the rum. Cheers, I said, all the best.

Catch ye later, said Gus.

I kept walking, ower the hill and across in the direction of the good chip shop. There were five takeaways in this wee neck of the woods; two chip shops, two kebabs and a chinese. Their lights cheered the place up. Young teams hung about the doorway, smoking and making comments, sometimes ye felt yer shoulders hunching, expecting a fucking brick. A guy I knew appeared from round a corner, coming towards me. I couldnay have avoided him even if I wanted to. He was alright but, Charlie, a bit of a wanderer. He would have been to *The New Dock* and was now heading to *The Ship*. From there he would catch a last pint in the place I just left. A wanderer, aye, but a creature of habit. At least ye could talk to him. Probably that was how he went from pub to pub. So he could get a conversation. Or else get left in peace. Ye could understand it. The worst way ye got a choice. That was what I was gony start doing. Only trouble is ye needed a few quid. Then too sometimes ye just couldnay be fucking bothered.

Alright Matt?

Aye no bad Charlie yerself?

Charlie slapped his hands the gether, breathed into the palms. Turning cauld, eh!

Aye there's a nip in the air.

He looked up at the sky. Time for the woolly jumpers. Then he clapped me on the side of the shoulder. Heh guess what? I've landed a start.

Have ye?

Charlie chuckled. Wait till I tell ye. I'm standing in the fucking *Hub*, me and a wee mate, having a couple of halfs. I nicks into Corals for a bet on the Sky night races, so we're watching them in the bar and all that passing the time, I mean it's no serious money man I'm just fiddling know I'm no fucking bothering. But I backs a winner; seven to one shot – a claiming race, bit of a step down in company ye know it'd been running in some no bad handicaps, Carole's Boy . . .

Carole's Boy aye; what a mile?

Mile and a quarter.

Step up in distance and aw eh?

Aye that's how I read it, plus with the all-weather and that ye know I thought aye it's got a fucking chance. Cut a long story short, I'm back in Corals collecting and I'm having a wee look at the next race; next thing a cunt bangs me on the shoulder; turns out it's a guy I know from years ago, a plumber, I used to do a bit of work with him, labouring and aw that, a bit of driving tae cause he had lost his licence – bevy merchant know – so I'm asking eftir his faimly and aw that; me and the wife and him and his wife, we used to pal about the gether, the women got on, the four of us used to hit that place down Cowcaddens, the place with the cabaret –

No *McGilligan's*?

McGilligan's aye, that's right. Mind that Saturday night lounge man it used to be good? Fucking soul bands the lot.

It was brilliant, me and Anne went aw the time. Ye're talking a while ago Charlie.

Aw I know man it's all changed to fuck, wait till I tell ye but, so the guy and that he asks me if I'm working cause they've just had to gie a cunt his jotters – disappearing off the job.

Hh! Fuck . . .

Aw I know, mental stuff, this day and age – cut a long story short but I dont have to tell ye . . . Charlie was waggling his shoulders now and he slapped his hands the gether: So ye up for it he says. Am I up for it I says ye fucking kidding!

What a turn!

What a turn! Matt, I fucking nearly forgot to lift my dough man I'm fucking telling ye! Charlie blew into his hands and rubbed them: Fucking luck eh! That's how it works but innit, ye back a winner then ye land a start.

Christ almighty.

Cunt wanted me in the morrow morning! I says no way man I need to get some fucking gear. I mean it's that fucking long Matt know? I've no even got a pair of boots! The way it's going I'll have to turn up in a pair of slippers; no unless the wife drops me a few quid. Fucking pyjamas man I'm no kidding ye.

Pyjamas!

Naw but ye know what I'm talking about.

Ye'll get a sub but Charlie.

Aw well I dont know about that so much, times have changed man – the money's no that good either by the way, I was surprised.

The building game's fucked but innit . . .

Och aye. It's been fucked for years. Mind you, I'm no grumbling.

Naw are ye fuck ye're out celebrating, quite fucking right!

Ach I'm always fucking celebrating man ye kidding! Charlie slapped me on the arm, rubbed his hands the gether, blew into them. He sniffed and glanced ower his shoulder.

I patted him on the back. I'll just get a bit of yer luck! I said.

That's aw it was Matt luck, pure and unadulterated.

Ach good on ye ya cunt.

Charlie grinned. What ye off up the road?

Aye.

Maybe see ye in-by later on?

Maybe.

Charlie nodded. Right, he said.

I watched him go, walking at his usual pace. Which was quite quick. I had noticed that before about Charlie. Heh Charlie! I shouted: Charlie!

He stopped.

If ye hear of anything . . . !

Aye nay danger Matt!

Just if ye hear!

He gave me a wave then carried on walking, one hand in his coat pocket, the other swinging by his side. There had to be something about it. A guy that walked quick. At least he didnay walk slow; so it meant ye werenay lazy, people saw ye werenay lazy. It was like ye were confident. Who was wanting to gie ye a job if ye werenay confident, if ye were

121

a loser, who wants ye if ye're a loser. Naybody. Nay fucking
wonder. Jesus christ; all important.

It was a fifteen-minute walk hame. I met Marie Reilly with
one of her lassies, they walked arm-in-arm. I passed them.
Aw right Marie! I said. She gave me a smile but didnay say
anything back. She had a couple of videos under her arm.

By the time I was going up the stair I was thinking the
worst. What was the worst? I didnay want to think about
it. Just something bad. So there was nay point. I would
hear about it soon enough, ping pong, one thing life taught
ye was how stupid it was to worry about things ye didnay
know for sure, things that might no even happen, nay point
in worrying about them.

I hung my jacket in the hall then lifted the phone but
didnay make the call, it was bad luck. In the bedroom I took
off the trousers, the coins scattering out the pockets when I
held them up to fold away. Every fucking time, the same. I
gathered it up, pulled on the pair of joggers I wore round the
house. I heard the music so I knew he was in, the boy. Doing
fuck knows what, lying on his bed probably. Staring out the
window, probably no even hearing the music. Sometimes ye
thought he was in a trance; but it wasnay dope, I knew that
for a certainty.

The lassies would be out someplace. Wherever. Whatever.
I chapped the door and shouted: Richard! It's da! Any word
of yer mother? She didnay phone did she?

Naw.

Where's yer sisters?

Out.

Nay messages at all?

Naw.

Nothing?

Naw.

122

Ye in bed?

I'm reading.

Did ye eat?

Aye.

I was about to ask what had he eaten but couldnay have
trusted myself. I went for a piss. Sometimes Anne was late.
Sometimes she didnay show when she said she would. No that
it bothered me; it wasnay her fault. Her family were talkers
and so was she. No so much a talker, she liked company. Fuck
aw wrong with that. Because I was out the habit didnay mean
she had to be. A couple of mornings ago, down the post office,
there was this elderly woman in front of me and she turned
round and started chatting. I didnay chat back. I couldnay. I
felt like I wanted to but I wasnay able. There was a whole
queue and it was me she spoke to. Fucking amazing. The one
person she chose. A nice auld woman tae. Her weans were
grown up and she was a grannie and aw that, maybe even
a great-grannie, I cannay mind. Probably her man was deid.
Probably years ago. That was the way it went. Out the blue,
he probably just dropped deid. The road goes on forever and
so does the women, they outlast every bastard.

A plane was passing, circling the airport. Back from some
holiday resort, a charter, it looked hell of a big.

There was a pot of soup. I made it at 4 o'clock. I wondered
whether to microwave a bowlful. Or else just wait till later.
The lentils were crusted round the side of the pot, I felt
like scraping it with a wooden spoon, making it smooth.
On the other hand. Plus there was the dishes, I still had
them to do.

But naw, I was hungry. I couldnay be bothered but, I
switched on the telly. It took time to heat up. I was
seeing Doreen again, she was turning to me, she had a
laugh on her face, she was wearing a jersey and a pair

123

of slacks or else maybe a skirt, but this big happy look. I didnay even have my eyes closed and there she was. That was my lassies, sometimes they gave me the exact same look.

Then later

Naybody was aboot hardly and I was hearing my ayn footsteps on the cobbles. I came out frae the back lane gon quite quickly but at the same time pacing myself. Somebody watching wouldnay know how far I had come, a couple of miles or just roon the corner. Ower my left arm was the coat, I had it folded – which didnay seem right somehow, even the wey I cerried it was wrang, I knew it; but what could I dae? Maybe if I had slung it across my shooder it would have looked merr the part, but I wasnay that bothered. I crossed ower the wee path up by the canal bridge. The grass was soaking wet and there was piles of litter scattered ower the grun and further on a couple of lumps of shite beside the fence, human shite, at least that was what it looked like. Some dirty bastard. Then another pile of rubbish stacked in among the ferns – including a stack of rubbers, like a gang of weans had fun a gross and startit blawing them inti balloons.

I waited afore heading up and along the canal bank cause ye never know. And frae there ye can see a good wey away. I kept at a fast walk, needing to get out of sight quickly, there was almost nay cover at all noo, no on this side, anybody looking from the road below would have spottit me a mile away fuck, easy. When I got to the lock I had the coat bundled up and gripped in my left hon. I stooped like I was gony tie my shoelaces but I was wanting to see if the coast was clear. This is a point it can be tricky, ye can be too impatient, or else forgetful, ye think ye're hame and dry. I was doubly careful cause of it, I knew other cunts had

fuckt up right at that very moment. I didnay care how long
it took, within reason. I had the message oot by the tip of
the handle. I let it drap and it went plopping doon inti the
rushes just oot frae the bank. I couldnay resist waiting an
extra second. Even daeing it I knew how stupit it was but
ye know the wey it goes, that funny feeling ye're gony see
it bounce back oot again, then go jumping alang behind ye,
and ye dont know it's there, no till whenever, whatever –
stupit – but yer heid's gon in all directions, the closer ye get
the merr nervous ye ur.

So ower the lock, and that good smell; for me anywey it's
a good smell, I know it's fucking detergent and aw that; but
there's something aboot it. Plus cause it's sae open, ye get
a breeze. Nay matter. I cerried on in the direction of the
Methodist Church. This route led me oot frae between two
gable-ends. I got there and then came a loud rattling noise,
a lorry. I stood still. It was a delivery wagon. The driver was
sterring at me. I gave him a nod but he didnay nod back.
For some reason that annoyed me, it really did, fuck you
ya bastard, I sterred back at the cunt. I cannay explain it,
fucking idiot bastard. Nay kidding ye but the smoke was
coming oot my ears. I dont know what the fuck it was to dae
with. Maybe gratitude or something. I know it's stupit and
there's nay reason behind it. Gratitude? I know. What can ye
dae but, ye're just telling it, getting it oot. It's best getting it
oot. Nay point letting it fester. Anywey, soon enough there
was nothing I wantit to dae. Nothing I felt I should be daeing.
Then I was walking. And I got this great feeling. It was cause I
had left the driver cunt. I had met him and had the wee minor
altercation, letting him see what I thought and aw that, and
then when it came to the crunch I just left him stonning, I
just fucking turned, no even smiling, nothing, I just fucking
turned, that was that, I left him stonning, I left him to get on

with it, his fucking deliveries. See if that hadnay happened, if the cunt hadnay reacted the way he had, I really dont think I would have got hame in the right frame of mind; something would have steyed unfinished. Definitely. It sounds shite but that was the wey it was. I felt strong as fuck. Mentally as well. It was June tae and that's something, the sky was fucking great, total blue. Ye felt like gon hiking or fucking climbing; maybe if ye had a bike, take yer stove and some grub.

I watch for signs all the time. The least oot the ordinary thing, ye're aye thinking this is the ane, this is the fucking ane, this is it. And see when it isnay! Hoh, jesus christ.

It doesnay matter aboot the coat. Curiosity killed the cat. So they say anywey.

Comic Cuts

These things always begin in a less than unexceptional manner. It's a case of grabbing the nettle. What else is there?
What else could there be? And I stress the 'could'. One
has to accept these things; if ye were to examine every last
detail, every last detail. Being speaking I was awake, but
weary, weary. I stared at the guy, having to concentrate
my mind, focus, focus, abracadabra. Then came a screech.
It was just the wooden chair I was sitting on. I had shifted
my seated position. Another sound, barely discernible, the
ticktick of a clock. Then too Vik's breathing, regular, not
snoring. My best mate, partner and mucker, he was stretched
out behind the kitchen table. He had terrible bony joints and
couldnay have been too comfortable. Mind you I'm no too
comfortable myself, I said, what is this? a wean's high-chair?
I'm fucking perched here. Nay wonder my back's sore!

The other guy – Rory was his name. I remembered it.
Amazing feat. Sometimes I find myself an incredible creature
– he was frowning at me. What's up? I said.

Ye were saying something.

I was saying a lot.

Well say it.

It's a lot.

I dont mind if it's a lot.

Now the door creaked open and Bill entered. I remembered him as well. He was giving me a right cheery smile.
Alright Colin? he said.

Aye.

The soup'll be another ten minutes.

I knew somebody mentioned soup in the recent thingwi, I just knew it.

Ye probably thought I went out to plant the vegetables!

I wasnay sure. Mind you, what if it had been a piece of flank mutton ye were looking for, know what I mean, London, never easy for sheep.

Too true.

No at this time of night it isnay.

It's fucking morning, said Rory.

What a stickler.

Bill chuckled. He sat down on a cushion near the fireplace. I'm quite hungry myself, he said.

No as hungry as me.

Ye were making a point, said Rory.

I was making a point. Mm. I wonder what point I was making?

It's fucking niggling me.

Right, aye, well, we're always subject to niggles, that's the nature of the endeavour. If ye look closely at anything niggles will emerge, factors that gnaw at ye, factors that take on a certain significance, a niggling significance. My back's really sore by the way. Sorry, where was I?

Niggling factors, said Bill, if they're significant.

Yeh, what if they are right enough. I find it best just to shrug, let it pass let it pass; life is difficult enough without all these needless proceedings beyond the present; trails-in-the-pursuit-of-understanding and so on, such trails are not so much dangerous as a form of mental blue-herring, put forth by the powers-that-be; what was is sufficient and what is will become so. Let it be shouted from every rooftop. These other points of reference are all very well.

Bill grinned. Formulate them at your peril.

129

Well said sir.

Formulate them at your peril!

Doubly well said sir

Ye were making a point, said Rory. I want to hear it. We all want to hear it. Even Vik, and he's fucking sleeping.

Vik's always sleeping, that's how he's the man ye see today.

Make yer point.

Mm. What kind of point was I making? Somebody mentioned soup in the not-too-distant past, it appears to have affected my concentration.

Was this soup homemade or out a tin? said Bill.

Such a settlement depends on the gods my son, if they perchance are smiling favourably upon one. Mayhap they are. Unless one has offended them. Willy nilly as it were yea though in the scheme of things, the chain of life's sweet mystereees.

Look, said Rory, ye made a statement.

Did I christ in my line of work that's an accusation. Ponder ponder. Mm, maybe it was a proposition, a form of argument.

Whatever.

Whatever. Ah, are you a religious guy by any chance?

Ha ha

Naw I just mean if ye have a propensity towards the erstwhile supranateeraal. One has to know where one has landed so-to-speak, the precise location, conceptually I'm talking about, otherwise . . . realms of irrational discourse and all that, know what I mean, religion, it's a second-order signifier.

Is that a fact.

Maist people think it's first-order

I suppose it depends, said Bill.

Rory scowled at him.

Naw but the guy's got a point.

Point! What fucking point? He's blabbing, he's just blab-bing.

Plus as well as that ye find about certain arguments, I said, that they arenay even worth the refutation; and I'm being honest with ye, especially in circumstances as of the present where one is so-to-speak carpeted, engaged by the beaks. We shouldnay take it personally. I never do, plus as well as that ye're aye having to remember it's one of these discussions.

Bill nodded.

Rory shook his head at him. See what I mean! he said. What discussions? What fucking discussions is he talking about! Eh, Colin, whatever yer name is, what discussions are ye fucking talking about?

Them, these yins, these yins here, the kind that take place in pubs around ten to twenty past seven on a wintry weekday evening towards the end of a very long afternoon drinking session. Ye know the ones I mean, these disjointed yet strangely coherent conversations where meaningful matters of the spirit are somehow raised from the long-dead data of base experience. Outside it's all dark and dismal. But so too is the inside, except it's that wee bit less so, owing to the reflected mellow sheen from the dust-covered bottles of guid auld Ooossskkii, lurking up there on the gantry, barely reminding us of its doughty though deadly presence. Or else ye've got it as of now, deeply into the wee a.m.s, that tricky period when the end of the carry-out doth approacheth, indeed hath patheth, pathethed away . . . drip drip . . . drip drip . . .

I made a plopping noise with my tongue on the roof of my mouth. Bill kept watching me for a wee minute then shivered. Alright? I said.

Ye're talking about the story of my life.

Och gie us a fucking break, said Rory.

Naw, honest.

Ah well Bill, I said, it's what happens. But dont worry about it, you've got said life under control. Or so it appears to me anyway, a veritable stranger; one who has so to speak landed in yer midst.

Bill shook his head.

Naw, ye're a positive guy, witness the soup, that's a positive move if ever I saw one.

He'll probably burn it, said Rory.

Naw I'll no, I never burn soup.

D'ye burn other things? I said.

Bill hesitated then smiled. Yeh.

So do I. That's exactly the point I'm making ye see cause then there's the music.

Bill nodded.

This is shite, said Rory, he knows fuck all about music.

Who me? I said.

Aye you, ye know fuck all about it.

My son it's not what ye know it's how, how ye know, the crux of the 21st century post-medieval intellectual position, as adopted by all religions and retail state-media outlets, let me tell ye boy this is the crux, thee crux, veritabeeleh

Ye said something earlier on. I'm still waiting to hear what it was. Ye gony tell us?

Aw christ aye nay bother, I was just saying what you were saying, that no matter what I think about the politics of a certain white english rockband some of their early recordings might be instances of perfection in the singing of rhythm and blues: all its rawness and that kind of stupendous stuff.

That's no what I was saying.

Ye sure? said Bill. It sounds a bit like ye.

Fuck off man.

Naw I've heard ye say things like that before.

Have ye fuck.

It's your kind of argument.

It isnay my kind of argument.

Well, verily brother I say unto you that it is hardly an argument at all, I said, not in the true sense of the term, its classical sense, the ways in which one may so to speak walk round an argument, nodding one's head at the bits that work, the bits that dont work . . . Heh is that fried onion and garlic I smell? Ye dont fool me Bill that's turmeric as well . . . sniff sniff, and correct me if I'm wrong, the merest twinkle of crushed cuminaah?

You better believe it!

A cordon-bleu tin right enough. Bill Bill Bill I lo'e ye dearly. But that smell always renders one helpless. I'm as a new-born babe, my brains are fucking addled, if not comatose.

Ye dont care for rock music then, is that what this is all about?

Beg pardon?

D'ye consider it inferior or something? said Rory, I'm talking about as a form of art.

Inferior?

Is that the point ye're making?

Sorry . . .

Is that the point? Eh? Is that yer fucking point?

Sorry, I said, my attention was genuinely arrested.

Rory stared at me.

Naw honest, I do apologise. I was all set to answer ye when my eye got caught by that there alarm clock perched on that there high shelf. See its face, obscured in a shadow of indeterminate extension cause unknown,

133

unless maybe through the ceiling in the upstairs flat lurks a full-blooded human entity whose presence is wont to cast itself spiritually through plaster board and joist beams and various other construction paraphernalia. Does such a supranateeral being exist, terra noviticus-a-um? Is there anybody in the upstairs flat? I said, That's what I want to know.

Nobody at all, said Bill, it's a bare attic

Bare attic. Christ, that's quite sexy

Bill chuckled.

Look, said Rory, ye made a statement there a wee minute ago about perfection.

Right ye are, that it just isnay possible to speak of perfection since the actual perception of it would perforce be filtered through the subject's knowledge that the person who wrote and perhaps even recorded the song originally was getting badly exploited by the white record companies and this means a slight niggling doubt would lurk in that knowledge the person had, no matter how uninformed; even if it was an ignoramus who made the statement, somebody who played music all their damn life and never wanted to find out anything about damn art, even for them – I'm saying even for them – it would still only exist as part and parcel of the actual perception, and the judgment as verbal effect of said deliberations so that the very notion of 'perfection', the very notion, would itself be called into question. So, fellow chaps, male muckers: there are definitely things that seem one thing whereas often they turn out to be another thing altogether, allioos alliee.

I'm ambiguous, is that what ye're saying, because I only do what I do in my spare time?

Ambiguous?

Ye're calling me into question, because I only play music part-time, ye're saying I'm ambiguous? Eh? Ye're saying I'm ambiguous?

Sorry, it's yer use of the word 'ambiguous', it's throwing me.

Am big u us

Aw right, aye; but as well as that ye see it's no necessarily a criticism. We have to accept different forms of ambiguity, as human beings, there's different ways we operate. Obviously it doesnay matter if I'm talking to a fool, a classified fool, restricting it to the clinical usage.

Now my train of thought was interrupted by Vik making a snoring sort of rattling noise, like his nostrils were jammed. Indeed this is what it was. His breathing apparatus was very fucking strange. There were other things about him too. All in all he was an amazing guy and I loved him but for the last few minutes his breathing had been discernible though he was not snoring, and there was a familiarity about it, like a sort of rattling, definitely. Yeh, we all want to die, but that isnay the point.

What? Bill frowned.

I looked at him.

Who's talking about dying? he said. Naybody's talking about dying. I dont want to die.

Maybe he does! said Rory.

I thought we all did.

What ye on about?

I've tried to die for years, I said, I used to lie down in streets hoping to get run ower by a fucking huge gigantic enormous big truck. It didnay work but.

Come on Colin, that isnay funny.

Naw Bill I've got to say it. Take Vik as a for instance, he's developed this habit of falling asleep. Yet it's only in awkward company. The point being there is only awkward company. That's what I cannay get him to understand. If it wasnay for women and music he would never wake up at all. It's the one thing that keeps him alive to the world.

That's two things, said Rory.

Of course it isnay, how long ye been involved in showbiz? Plus as well as that, ever notice how women show a marked preference for guys like him?

Guys like who?

Guys like Vik.

Guys like Vik?

Aye.

Get to fuck.

It's true.

I agree, said Bill. I've seen it myself when he's been jamming in with us, like the night, that lassie with the red hair, she couldnay take her eyes off him.

I wouldnay say that, said Rory.

Och come on. Whatever it is Vik's got, a kind of . . . I dont know. What d'ye call it again Colin?

Gangularity.

Gangularity, aye, that's right; these big skinny fuckers, all elbows and bones, all jutting out.

Thumbs and kneejoints.

Right.

Women seem to cave in whenever they appear on the scene.

I know!

Rory said, It's no as simple as that.

I think it is, I said, speaking personally, I've never been able to forgive them for it, women I'm talking about, it's a thing about them, especially beauteous women, bounteous women, I mean how come it's them especially? There's a guy I know doing great analysis on the topic. Weighty but I've got to say, as topics go, most weighty.

Rory sighed.

Okay, what I was saying earlier, I mean it in the sense that the subject in order to make a judgment must rely on his or herself and that that judgment must also be filtered through this one person so therefore, I mean to say, how can it possibly be other than relative: and if that is the case then perfection just cannay come into it, we cannay even entertain the notion since the very idea itself is reliant on the existence of reason, in other words more than one person is necessary; this being a prerequisite of reason, a dialogue, that more than one person has to be there.

What if the person cannay talk? said Rory.

Bill smiled. Well what if it isnay a person at all?

Rory frowned at him.

Mind you but Bill a lot of people get turned off by mental highjinks, they have a fear of it, almost a phobia; matters of the intellect do their fucking nut in, that kind of activity, it makes them sleepy, it makes them sleepy . . . I glanced at Rory: Did you yawn there by the way?

What?

I was wondering if ye yawned.

When?

There the now, when ye were rolling the joint.

Naw.

Ye sure? Cause we deny such things at our peril.

Is that a fact. Ye're making a point: make it.

Making a point?

Make the fucking point.

Me?

You, aye.

I think ye were, said Bill.

Yeh okay, but in truth and verily I say unto you, meta-arguments are always unforgivable, even in unrelaxed company. Of course there's usually something in around the root, a principle that might be cornered, if we put our minds to it, if we just dig around and expose the fucker. And whatever that underlying thing is, if we find it, it could save our bacon. Personally I know we're close but at the same time we shouldnay worry about failure I mean to say who finds it easy following complex propositions at this time of night?

Yeh, said Rory, especially when it's morning.

Especially when it's morning.

Listen, earlier on you said artists have smug attitudes.

Surely no?

Ye did, said Bill.

Me!

You, aye.

Christ, I shook my head, but Vik's breathing was getting in the way of my thoughts. Ye feel like sticking a handkerchief ower his nose and forcing him to blow. Course ye'd only wake him up.

What's wrong with that? said Bill.

He'll just want to know when the soup's ready.

Ten minutes.

D'ye mean ten minutes or else another ten minutes?

I thought ye werenay really hungry!

Who me?

That's what ye said earlier.

Christ Bill you've some imagination; if I did I was just being polite, a good guest.

Yeh, ha ha, said Rory.

I take it good guests are rare in this part of the world?

Unknown fucking entities.

What part of the world is this anyway? What kind of

138

world I should say. I hope it's no an enclave of out-skirts.

It sure is, said Bill.

Southern outskirts?

Now ye've got it.

God love us.

It didnay occur to us before we moved in. But once ye're here ye're here.

It's no a place ye would visit in a hurry but eh! I said. Not freely, not by choice, not in a fucking month of fucking Sundays.

Dead right, said Rory. Except you have done.

Yeh, that's what I get for being a one-man roadie.

Where Vik's guitar goes you go eh?

I could tell ye a tale or two.

I bet ye could, prattle fucking prattle.

Just stating the general case old chap, indicating the timeless discrepancy between it and the particular; take for example hunger, one could be hungry; there again one could be out on one's feet so-to-speak verging on extinction, as for example Vik, half swazzled with the drink, not just dying in the sense that life amounts to a slow throe in that direction, but soon to be dead. His breathing, listen to his breathing.

What ye on about now?

Wheesht a minute, just listen, it's a nostril pile-up. It isnay healthy. He needs a drink of water, warm water, crystal clear and pure water. Ever regarded an animal?

I used to have a Dobermann pinscher.

Cats are better, just notice the way they stare at slow dripping taps, the intense way they concentrate on them, each drip's a phenomenal occurrence . . . incredeeblay, drip drip drip drip drip drip drip drip. What a world that must be, the world of cats. Never mind dogs, they might be big but so what, you're no big, I'm no big, but Vik, he's big, yer man, he's a big bastard; nevertheless and all the same there he is lying there, dead to the world, non compos mentis, out the fucking gemm.

What ye talking about? Eh?

Me?

Ye said something there about Vik.

I didnay say nothing.

About him dying or something, what the hell was it?

Pardon?

What was it ye said about him?

I wouldnay have said nothing about him. No when the guy's sleeping I wouldnay. Christ almighty, Vik, he's my mucker, my fucking mate.

Come on Rory, ye're no gony talk behind a guy's back! Bill shook his head.

I'm no talking behind naybody's back. It's him for fuck sake he's just eftir saying Vik's dying.

Och naw he didnay.

Aye he fucking did; that was what he said there a wee minute ago.

Och he was kidding.

Kidding! How do ye kid about a thing like that! He's supposed to be the guy's mate for christ sake.

So are we.

I fucking know we are, that's the point I'm making!

Bill winked at me. What was it ye actually said there again Colin?

Well being honest I was just thinking aloud.

Right . . .

The thing is but if we are talking it's us that's doing it, it's what us are talking about, and it's that 'what', that's what makes it the more complicated; see as far as I'm concerned

140

it's psychological, ye might think ye've got the reasoning power to defeat any bastard on any subject whatsoever – the origin of rhythm and blues, scholastic philosophy, terrorism and the indigenous subject, the theory of hydraulics – doesnay matter; it's just that concentration, that damn concentration, bane of one's existence, and it's got nothing to do with intoxicants, self-produced or whatever. Although having said that, sometimes I meet people and their heads and shoulders seem to be rising and approaching ever closer, closer and closer. Ever get that?

Yeh, yeh, I do, yeh.

Fucking wild innit!

Bill chuckled.

Get to fuck man, said Rory.

Naw, said Bill, it's right enough.

It strikes me the drip drip syndrome isnay entirely inappropriate Bill would ye say?

I would.

The dawning recognition?

Peraventure!

Peraventure; exactimon my boy exactimon. Once I laid me down upon the street, I tried to fade away; to no avail but to no avail. Imagine it, I couldnay even fade away.

I know the feeling!

It's like warm rooms, sooner or later ye have to leave them, I'm talking about when they urnay yours, ye can never just stay there, not indefinitely; and it's exactly the same with people ye love. Take women as a for instance . . .

Vik groaned awake.

See that chaps, the deeply-natured structure of the psyche's darker recesses! This guy's a walking wonderland.

What do you know about women? said Rory.

Never seen it?

What?

Ye've never seen it?

Seen what?

Uch it doesnay matter

Seen what?

It doesnay matter, no if ye've no seen it.

What's he talking about? said Rory.

Bill smiled, shook his head.

What ye trying to say that I've missed something?

Not at all, I said, but take Vik here

You take him!

Well I've took him.

Who's took me? said Vik. People are aye fucking taking me, I'm sick of it. He groaned and scratched himself. Jesus christ man my back, it's breaking!

That's what ye get for gon to sleep on the floor.

What were you saying there? said Rory.

Me?

You, aye.

I was saying something?

About women.

Mm, right, well, aye, the female of the species, mmm, how ye can see that wee something in her, the sort of security she has, in the fact of one's temporariness. Women Vik, I'm talking about women, as if ye hadnay noticed.

In respect of the vagaries thereof?

What else?

Are these vagaries eternal?

Ye see that chaps a syllogism, what an embarrassment this guy is.

Naw but Colin I was in a deep mental crevice when awakened so rudely.

Nay excuses.

Honest, I had to crank myself back into consciousness. Clinging on by the skin of my whatever-ye-call-thems . . .

Ye've aye had mighty fingertips.

I had entered a cave wherein shadows lurk.

We've all been in that selfsame fucking cave, seen the selfsame fucking shadows, come on, that's nay big deal!

Naw but this time it was really something Colin ye want to have been there.

How do I know I wasnay! Were these shadows fiery?

They were.

Jesus christ man the auld fiery shadows of passion!

Bill was nodding. Yeh!

Come on, said Rory, dont let him off the hook, he was making a point about women.

Was I?

Aye.

Mm.

We're all waiting, yawned Vik.

Et tu ya bastard! So, I was making a point . . . it was to do with women, about or concerning, to wit or to woo . . .

Aye! Bill was nodding again. Right Colin, he said, right, I think I know, I think it was to do with eh like eh I mean how eh it's just because the woman, she knows ye've got to be going, sooner or later, you as male I'm talking about . . . the woman, she knows ye have to be going soon . . . you, that ye urnay a permanent fixture . . . You as males, us, we urnay a permanent fixture, we're never . . . we're just . . . it's that kind of thingwi, it's that, it's that that makes her the eh . . . that gives her the eh . . . somehow ye know it's . . . it's the one thing, that one thing . . .

That gies her the spring in her step?

Yeh, yeh.

The bounce in her being?

That's it, aye.

As she studies her reflection in the mirror, critically, objectively . . . Or subjectively eh, who knows with women!

Right.

Yeh, said Vik and then chuckled, that smile at the edge of her mouth . . .

Even when ye lay one's hand upon her shoulder, the very act, the very selfsame.

Yeh.

Bill sighed.

Amazing stuff, said Vik.

Who knows with women, said Bill.

Yeh! Vik slapped his hands together and made a smacking sound with his lips. I'm gasping for a drink.

Just as well there isnay one, I said, ye want to see how red are the veins in your eyes. Honest. I've never seen a pair of peepers like that in my entire existensus.

What's up with them? said Bill.

He's led a shifty existence, that's what's up with them. The eyes is where it comes out, ye cannay hide it from them, the auld peepers. And we all look into them, that's the beauty of it. So ye cannay hide it from us either.

My boy, said Vik, why have you forsaken me!

Dont you start, said Rory, matey here's been doing my brains in.

Colin's a powerful presence, there's no denying it. Vik yawned again then started laughing before the yawn ended.

Aw naw, I said.

I've got to tell ye but.

Naw ye've no.

Aye I have.

It's his dreams, I said to the other two, there's a certain lassie haunts them. Well a woman, she's fully fledged.

Vik I hope ye're no gony embarrass us! Yer eyes have went glassy.

Naw but Colin her blouse, as per usual it was open, and she wasnay wearing a bra, this habit she has of doing that, so her bosoms there hanging out, a slight swing to them, the nipples low and to the sides, and the outline of her ribs, she being quite thin not counting her bosoms of which there were two, there were two, I stared at them . . .

Aye ye've got to, said Rory and chuckled, then he went silent.

It was like an absurd extension of myself . . .

What else could it be! I said.

What else could I be?

You, you could be anything, anything.

I was anything; at the same time I was nothing.

Of course, that's the beauty of the entire kit and caboodle, the entire bounteous nature of this limitless and infinite universe, this home from home for the living breathing free spirit, the unshackled agent.

I was nothing. Nothing.

At the same time ye were something.

I just needed to get shot of the thingwi, the damn fucking eh . . . I needed to get rid of it, rid of it

That auld story.

Just get rid of it.

I know.

Yeh but at the same time Colin I was so aware of it, exactly that, how old a story it was, and there was me, an integral part of the continuum, in toto, I was as an instrument, verily.

Uch, forget women's bodies. We're no gony get one and that's that.

What ye talking about? said Rory.

We're being metaphysical, said Vik.

145

What?

It's just like what me and you were saying a wee minute ago re rock music and a certain white english upperclass band who apparently are or were perfection in that medium.

Are yous fucking still talking about that! said Vik.

I wasnay, said Rory.

Tis an interesting topic, I said, take for instance once ye start on about voice which all you artiste squad have a habit of doing – no just part-time ones either. Aye Vik even you, you're included.

What ye dragging me into it for?

He's dragging us all into it! said Bill.

Because yez're all musicians, part-time or whatever, it doesnay fucking matter. So okay, I'm no wanting to tell tales out of school but if it has to be faced then it should be faced, yousa culpa, that critical point being made earlier on concerning voice, the veracity thereof. What ye said Vik . . .

Me?

Aye you, what ye said – it was just after that wee jam session yez all had doon the boozer – I dont know exactly how ye meant it but if it was to do with the original recording artist, the guy who wrote the song and perhaps made that first studio-based version and certainly the first performance whenever that was, if it was his actual voice ye were referring to.

It wasnay

It wasnay?

Naw.

So what was it then?

It was his individual existent being.

Exactly! I snapped my fingers. So verily it becomes pertinent to inquire what it is ye're applauding I mean to say what the fuck are ye actually applauding if it's the white upperclass rock band ye're applauding like I mean it was Joe Turner or somebody christ if that's what ye're trying to say about them, that fucking band – their name escapes me – I mean is it the perfection of technique or what because if so the argument doesnay hold unless we're back to the animal world and Shakespeare and making a case for interesting monkeys, that auld chestnut about the machine creating great musical inventions once we get the programme sorted out, which is just naive claptrap, but if so then voice is surely eliminated and I would have thought any artiste worth his or her salt would back me up on that one, at least intuitively jees it seems to me obvious Vik for christ sake come on, even part-time musicians, actors and others of that ilk.

Some voices should be eliminated altogether, said Rory.

Aye of course, of course, I agree with that as well, given that usually it gets excused by extraneous stuff to do with inauthentic credos, instead of the reality, the base.

Yeh. Bill was frowning, now he nodded his head: Time and the movement of matter.

Exactly. Having said that the use of the term 'extraneous' needs to be clarified, and where clarification is a major concern you'll find that time is itself being exploited.

Yeh.

Mind you it can further be said there is always something nauseating and maybe sad – and I'm talking about on a good day – when ye hear young singers from these ordinary working-class communities assume the american singing voice which is as bad as these upper-class RP voices of the 1950s they all tried so hard to eradicate, not just at the BBC.

Sir Alec fucking whatsisname, the royal family.

What? said Rory.

Spot on Bill although ye forgot about the church, the old pulpit, the power thereof. To hell with meritocracy son know what I'm talking about? Eh? Rory . . .

What?

I dont know if you actually sang as well as played that lead guitar all night long christ it would drive ye nuts when the PA's askew, not that it was the night as far as I know, speaking as a non-player, it's only a for instance, I'm just saying if it had been, as a hypothesis, but if it was you I heard singing then I would have thought ye'd agree that there's nothing worse than hearing a singer go straight into the language of an alien culture to sing a boy-meets-girl song, the situation occurring in locations like Oklahoma or Tulsa, Tuscon or Montana, with reference to home-home-on-the-range, highheel sneakers, hotdog stands, drive-in movies and James Dean, Hank and old Lefty, Muddy and Bo, all that kind of crap; I'm not being sarcastic by the way, I'm just telling it like it is.

Ye're making a point matey so make it.

Bill said, Rory he's fucking made the point.

Well he can make it again then cant he. What you laughing at Vik?

Me?

Ye're fucking laughing.

Hush, I said, it's not a measure of things that one art is more easily perfected than another.

Blessed be the peacemakers my son. Vik bowed his head, clasped his hands together. Anger is to be treasured, yea though it's gunsmoke at dawn, duels to the bitter death, we maun treasure our anger.

And let loose our rage only in meaningful spurts, I said, take the art of driving a train, given it doesnay compare with the art of the lead guitar. Although mind you, the art of the big bass drum . . .

Aye fuck you, said Rory, so what do you do yerself? What do ye actually fucking work at?

Sorry I thought ye knew; I'm in the State Security Service same as Vik, internal or external – I seem to remember being asked the same question on a previous occasion by the way . . . unless maybe it was a previous existence.

It wasnay a previous existence, said Vik. Wait a minute, did we come straight here from the pub?

We did.

Yez've been here ever since, said Bill. We're throwing yez out once the soup's been served.

The soup's been served, did ye hear how he phrased that? Already he's put it into the past tense. I'm telling ye, I'm no sure if I believe in the existence of this soup.

What about one's nose? said Vik.

Circumstantial evidence, no worth a fuck. This soup's like the good auld dead sheep, even if it existed we wouldnay find it. Aye me old shipmate, auld mucker o mine. Ye realise where we are by the way?

I do not.

Tell him

Our flat, said Rory.

In the deepest south of this city, said Bill, the outer outskirts.

My god! said Vik.

Yeh, what a place to die ya lucky bastard; all these wonderful wee redbrick houses with their wonderful wee doors and brass knockers.

Is it still snowing?

Still snowing! My gaaad!

Aw fuck naw.

Aye and yer mate's wearing sandals! said Rory.

Och well he always wears sandals, he's known for it, snow or muddy swamps, it makes nay difference.

I'm a bit of a legend in the old shoe department, which is why soup is the great temptress. And rightly so, being a vital component to life's centrality, especially when ye've that long walk home awaiting. Smack bang in the middle of said elementals, that's what I'm talking about.

If I dont get home soon I'll fucking collapse.

Ye have collapsed Vik this is you on the up and up.

How the bleeding hell do we get home but that's the question . . . He crossed over to the window, pulled back the curtains. Jesus christ it's a winter wonderland! A veritable fucking winter fucking wonderland!

It be lying deep? I said.

Deep! Vik opened the window and stuck his head out.

Fuck sake! said Rory.

Fresh air, oxygenus. Life life life! Vik was breathing in exaggerated motions. This is amazing, he gasped, amazing.

Ye can actually see them from here, I said.

What?

Look, ye can actually see them, the auld corpuscles, they're haring through the guy's brains. Vik I can actually see the electrical tensions, they be twanging through the ether ma boy, ye can feel them, actually feel them

God's murmur . . . Vik sighed. Just like the good bishop reported.

Are the clouds faintly visible? I said.

Come and see!

Naw, tell me.

Yea and suchlike, they are faintly visible.

What about the vapours, their viscousness?

Aye.

Bastard, they aye destroy the damn calculations. Ye sure?

Verily brother: we have arrived at that dark dark blue stage; soon the watery sun will be on the horizon; and the snow might freeze, there again it might not.

Who can tell with snow.

Rory said, Come on Vik, shut the fucking window!

It's true enough, said Bill, snow goes its own way, Colin's right.

Yeh, but are there cracks in the sky, that's the real question, I said, the one that never gets asked, not by the academics, not by no cunt, naybody at all, they always dont ask that yin – too fucking feart so they are.

Cracks in the sky, said Vik, he does know the ones that count. A chap would wish for an apt rejoinder, one of these weighty epigrams.

Preferably in the Latin?

Absafuckinglootely. I dont know how ye manage it but when it comes to broken spokes in the wheel of life.

Thanks Vik.

Ye're a fucking trier man I'll say that for ye.

At least make the effort, that's what I always say. I make a point of it. I set out from A to B and fuck what comes in the middle, it's a watchword of mine.

Ye talking about the entire kit and caboodle?

I certainly am.

Astoniensus. Just breathe in.

Yeh.

Bill nodded.

What yez fucking on about? said Rory.

It is like a breath, said Bill. Ye can feel it . . .

The wind's fucking blowing in that fucking window, that's what ye can feel. Come on Vik, shut it for fuck sake.

Ah ye're a hard man.

151

It's freezing man I'm freezing.

Vik closed the window.

Life forces, I said, one knows intuitively, unless lacking the necessary spark

Twas ever thus, said Vik. Mind you, a general unwilling-ness can often exist. And of course you've a habit of saying things ye shouldnay.

At the same time I'm a hard nut to crack, especially if I'm waiting for a bowl of soup. What say you Bill?

It's coming.

Ye sure?

I'm sure.

I think I'll enter a reverie to pass the time, either that or a monastery.

I know how ye feel, said Bill, I'm just thinking about things myself.

Right.

A bit of me feels like hearing a joke.

What kind of a joke?

Charles Dickens.

Charles Dickens yeh.

I was thinking about what you said a wee minute ago about the absence of flank mutton, and then tae I was thinking about how far we are from Smithfield Market, if there was flank mutton to be had, if we went, I mean these days, the ones we're in now: or else if the whole thing's died out, and if it hasnay, if it hasnay, what then? Know what I mean?

Sure.

Just if the whole thing's died out.

I'm getting the picture, said Vik.

Well it's straightforward, I said, all these wee higgledy-piggledy buildings with the staircases outside. Ye see them stretching to the moon like in the movie with auld Fagin creeping up the stairs. Is that right Bill?

Yeh, a whole possee of people.

The merry band of youthful thieves. Leading them across the heaving morass of human jetsom and slimesum, like one of those fairy-tale castles in the sky, spanish yins, and then too with yer man, I'm talking about yer man . . .

The good Mister Sanchez, said Vik.

Windmills flailing, I said, dear god in Govan, Smithfield's, they'll be serving foamy pints accompanied by sizzling bacon and eggs any minute. Vik ma boy if we had the poppy we could walk it from here and maybe purchase a slap-up breakfast. Pints of luscious guinness and full plated fry-ups jees, imagine the scene. Maybe the porters would do us a deal and chip in a few pounds of best rump steak, a score of beef link sausages.

Foamy pints and sizzling bacon, said Vik.

But without the poppy . . .

Without the poppy . . . No man's land

We can but dream.

Peraventure, said Bill.

I did try it once when poppy had I none, it just wasnay on although the guy I was talking to, he was alright, an auld hand at the game, worked the market all his days. Aye and his grandmother before him, a genuine Bow Bells cockney, the sprightly article – it's even possible she knew Charles Dickens.

Bullshit, said Rory.

I'm only repeating what the guy said, as far as he said it, given it's difficult not to believe genuine auld guys like him, the salt of the earth and so on, he drank in the *Dirty Duck* or whatever ye call that boozer just down from the tourist trap

The thingwi, said Vik

Yeh, he tried to help out when these racist bastards behind the bar put the block on me saying I wasnay a worker and wasnay to get served – no just that, I wasnay even talking the full article, nineteen to the shilling, that was what they said! I mean what the hell would they know anyway? poncing about bowing and scraping to aw they tablefuls of city-gents, aw in for a curer, topping up the brandy & port before hitting the stock exchange, transforming thriving communities into wasted outposts of dereliction.

Ye need the bloodstained overalls for that game, said Vik.

Ye certainly do and that's what they carry in their brief-cases.

Aw aye, said Bill, right enough.

They wouldnay get served down Smithfields without them. That auld guy had one as well.

But it suited him, said Vik, he cut a dash.

This is crap, said Rory.

Some parties have got style but it's a matter of course. He was one such party. I'll never forget him, that auld butcher and his kindness to a peripatetic, an itinerant, a foreign stranger, friendless and alone in the world. What a sight for sore eyes the same man; a veritable Wackford Squeers of a fellow.

That's exactly it, said Bill.

What the fuck ye on about? said Rory.

What I was thinking about earlier on, Colin's got it.

Ye kidding!

Rory, I said, there can be many effects and only the one cause. Truly, very many effects from these singular mysterious causes, blatantly obvious causes, even discrete causes, none of which are admitted into the scheme of things, none at all.

And that by design, said Vik, yea unto the very valley. An illustration would be welcome.

Okay, well let me tell ye, it's about peculiar phenomena,

as if ye didnay know, and I include each last man amongst us in this, given we remain sensible to verbal percepts: to be specific it was one year ago to this selfasame very day, give or take a month.

When ye were hitching? said Vik.

Just returned from.

You were hitching! said Rory.

Traversing a continent adjacent to this yin, yeh.

Bill laughed and rubbed his hands together.

Naw Bill honest, and everywhere I landed there was this confrontation with the CNN news. Nay kidding ye. The people living there, the indigenous populace, they had all these honeycomb wee dwellings in the mountains wherein they've eked their living for nigh on three millennia, their ancestors before them. So I'm standing there marvelling at the spectacle when all of a sudden this guy in a cool suit starts chasing me up and down mountains, no kidding ye, up and down mountains, trailing me over dusty offbeaten paths and highrise peaks, all on the offchance I would inform of my activities for the folks back home, and this guy bringing up the rear, a technician chappie, with this big fucking gigantic huge fucking thingwi in his hands.

Arch boomer, said Vik.

Where is it ye were? said Rory.

Distant. I was wearing these here sandals at the time; in fact that was where I burst the damn buckle, going up a mountainous path with layer upon layer of crumbling larva larvae feminine, stones so-called, but I knew it wasnay stones, aw naw, that's one thing it definitely wasnay.

Yeh. Vik started snapping his fingers.

It was the crust-infested last resting place of tribilliolorum generations of reptilious wee hideous insects.

Yeh.

Crustaceous yins. Fucking millions of them man no kidding ye. Millions upon millions upon millions.

Yeh.

I know what ye're saying, said Bill, it's like how we're brought up as children.

Yeh, Vik still snapping the fingers.

If people would just stick to their own location . . .

Yeh.

Scotland, Wales, the Caribbean, Africa, the Indian sub-continent, regional England, Ireland, South East Asia, the Hebrides . . . Instead of coming to this land of the free.

Yeh.

He's no saying that at all! said Rory

If they just stuck closer to home, if they could just stick to that . . . then, their fights, their fights and struggles, they would be shared; they would have their topics in common; bad housing and the lack of recreational activities.

Spot on Billy ma boy, coffins that fit rather than the other way about.

Yeh, said Bill, and we know about coffins.

You better fucking believe it, said Vik.

Shut up, said Rory.

We do but.

Ye used to work in hospitals didnt ye?

That's right Colin. See what we discovered, about bodies, they're being mysteriously drained of life's fluid.

Flu-ids, I said, correction.

Fluids?

Yeh. Tell them Vik.

Well okay, ye see in a medical journal we read recently in the mess there was up-to-date terrorist research indicating there may be several varieties. Even in people's teeth; this is also where they're discovering fluids. These bright young

156

research think-tank assistants, some of them are okay, they get grants from capitol hill in respect of relevant findings, they're doing all this grand and exciting work, eg. is political dissent genetic? that this and the next thing. I passed the journal onto Colin once I had read it. Private-sector think-tanks, he's got a thing about them.

Too true, I said, but god strike me when I read about the findings in question I couldnay believe my fucking peepers. The same goes for him. In fact that was how he dragged me into it, to verify if said peepers were playing up.

But they werenay, said Vik.

They certainly werenay, and flu-ids was the outcome.

Colin's good at medical findings

Pooh pooh, I said, it's just a pastime

Naw but ye dae put things to the test, that was how ye got a start in the agency. See guys he thought he had failed the interview. How wrong can ye be.

Mind you but Vik I made the age-old error, I based my inference on the subjective.

The teeth of the people scenario.

The teeth of the people scenario, exactly. What we're saying about pleural fluids but Bill, never mind it's classified it's all on file, a fact of dental record.

Not much you dont know, said Rory.

Vik said, On the subject of hospitals he's good, hospitals and state-security, mine's music and women.

Heh as a matter of interest, I said, an elderly lady was telling me she was down the medical centre just the other afternoon and the place was hoaching with poor craturs, most of them dying, out on their feet. Rude health has become a luxury, not just for the rude masses, that was what she said to me.

Yeh, said Vik, I know that selfsame elderly lady, she's alive and kicking this very minute, she was this morning

157

anyway, I saw her down the Old Kent Road. Her daughter is extra-special by the way. Linda's her name. She wears seamless garments.

The beautiful Linda. Heh what's this! I said, my foot having just kicked into something solid but circular. A fucking bottle on the floor! Brandy! Threequarters full as well! I lifted it up and brandished it. Look at this!

Where did that come from? said Bill.

Who knows. It fucking seems one can fucking stumble upon cargoes perchance willy-nilly, unfuckingplanked so-to-speak. Mind you, in that selfsame manner of speaking, it was hiding under the settee.

Dont look at me, said Rory.

Not at all not at all, I'm just oh so pleased to have found the fucker.

Glasses! called Vik.

Bill laughed. Some life!

It is, said Vik, it's wonderful, one can find bottles of brandy at all hours of the morning. All we need now's a certain guy to pass the other stuff occasionally.

Definately, I said.

What? said Rory.

Nothing, said Vik while making a smoking gesture with his fingers to his lips.

I thought we had done it aw in? said Bill

What? Rory was frowning.

Vik winked at him, Ye've been hogging that fucking blaw all night ma boy gie us a break

Naw I've no christ I've hardly any left.

Aye well some things last forever if naybody uses them.

Ah Vik, I said, Vik Vik.

What?

Let's enjoy it while we can.

Life?

Life.

Bill finished pouring the drinks and passed them round. Brandy's a great invention, he said, alcohol itself, really, when ye think about it.

In truth, said Vik, yea and verily. Ever wonder how we manage to get about on the planet without it? Bloody incredible so it is.

Totally, I said, I mean ye feel like being expansive but yer energy is sapped until finally one is tossed out into the cold blue yonder. And ye might be starving never mind gasping for a drink man I'm talking about starving. In fact ye are starving, ye're so very very starving. So exceedingly starving: so exceedingly starving ye huvnay a square ounce of thermal opposition left, no to face these damn elements, they're all ower the place. Then the knowledge hitting ye, there is no respite, not from the icy needles. And nor after that from the icy blanket which is set to fall about one's shooders. Folding itself round ye in the tightest most snugly secure wrap one could imagine, way beyond the strange cosiness of a run-of-the-mill straitjacket.

Now ye're talking, said Rory, straitjacket – ever wore one?

Often, said Vik.

What a surprise.

Ye know what's a surprise to me? I said, it's like every time ye hear a part-time artiste in a part-time band of players a whole world is taken for granted; that's what I mean, an entire world, similar to a closed-entry system but no quite, because it's more than that, and the only person that doesnay know it is the artiste himself, especially when he doubles up as lead guitar. It's like a subtext.

Precisely, said Vik, I've always said that. Shake, I'm Vik

159

I'm Colin.

Bill was smiling at us.

Boy meets girl, I said to him, it's fundamental to rock music. And to most art, it's one of the paradoxes.

Here we go with the bullshit blethering claptrap, said Rory.

Naw, said Vik, the paradoxes central to rock music, that's what Colin's talking about; boy meets girl, boy loses girl, girl finds boy, boy goes in the huff; girl apologises, her guilt increases, he lives happily ever after, we dont find out what happens to her; the kind of everyday storyline ye find in hollywood movies. The problem is ye've got to keep singing them for the rest of yer life and then for fuck sake ye wake up one morning and ye're forty years of age – forty years of age – and still wearing jeans. That's how I packed it in.

Come off it.

Bill said, It's true what he's saying but Rory, it happens to a lot of folk, ye want to sing adult songs about adult experiences but it's too late and ye find ye cannay.

Crap, if ye want to sing ye sing.

It's no as simple as that.

Aye it is.

Maybe it's just there's a knack, I said, and you've got it. Eh Vik, maybe he's got it and you've got it still to discover.

Said knack?

Said knack, still to discover. In the not so dim and distant future, or else afterwards, who knows, maybe ye've a life still to come.

Perish the thought.

Perish the thought! But the last person that says that to me was an English teacher, I remember her well; some apparition, she wore a brightly coloured cardigan with two buttons missing, but my my my could she mark an essay. I dont think she even knew what a seamless garment looked like.

Slainte, said Vik, here's to peace, wealth and security, the eternal verities.

Where does he get them? said Rory.

It's the time of night, I said, plus he's only stating the obvious, and we should treasure the obvious; in fact the obvious requires treasuring.

Rory stared at me. So what is it ye actually do in the State Security Service matey?

Matey! I smiled at Rory and said to Bill: I feel like gieing old thingwi here a wee pat on the muzzle. I'll rephrase it, I feel like gieing him a kiss

I'm asking ye a question, said Rory. What do you actually do?

My best.

Yeh, I knew ye'd say that.

I knew ye knew.

Did ye really?

Yeh ye see there's a lot of interesting phenomena about if ye want to behold them; and then if ye want to express yer thoughts about them, yer beliefs relative to them, whatever. If ye dont then good luck, who wants to set down laws; especially about phenomena.

Vik grinned. You're a devilish wee besom.

I am.

So I take it ye listen to a lot of rock music? said Rory.

In the auld days especially, aye, I did, it was a thing we done when we were at college, or university, I forget which one. Mind you a couple of the folk we listened to were dead. Except if they were white, if we listened to them, they had to be not dead. That even includes Elvis Presley.

Elvis Presley, said Rory, I find that interesting.

I knew ye would.

I knew ye knew.

He is dead, said Bill.

Yeh but no to them, all these students Bill this is the fascinating thing about it, that's what I'm talking about, they all think he's alive and kicking ass somewhere in Atlanta, Georgia, leading some remote bunch of christians on behalf of a covert arm of state in some sweet-smelling field-training camp, direct representative of the people's champion here on earth, hallelujah.

Ye're talking about fascism?

About art, art and students, how it relates to existence, not yer own existence but somebody else's, somebody far away from ye. In fact the farther away the better.

Ye talking about the generality?

The farther away the better.

Bullshit, said Rory. Hey – Colin – is that yer name?

Bullshit, yeh. Har har har. Rory . . . ?

What?

Hallelujah.

Fuck off.

Naw seriously but Bill like I'm saying, it's politics; a perfect example of the exploitation that goes on throughout the entire art industry and that includes the so-called artistes; all upfront blatant as well, and yous guys . . . well, there's no much more one can add.

Vik smiled. Slainte! He swallowed his brandy immediately then sighed and gazed at mine. A glow has entered one's being, he said.

Yeh well restrain yer peepers, said I, they be devouring me drink.

There's a last couple of drops in the bottle, said Bill.

Vik shook his head. I wouldnay stoop so low.

Naw go ahead, said Bill.

I'll feel so guilty.

You've never felt guilty in yer life, I said.

Listen to who's fucking talking!

Bill passed Vik the bottle.

Well only because we're waiting for the soup, said he, opening it up and squeezing it dry. Slainte again. Here's to ye lads.

Heh Vik, said Rory, I thought ye were getting off with her earlier on.

Getting off with who?

That red-headed babe.

Red-headed babe, I said, this is humiliating.

She had a boyfriend, said Vik, he was in the bar.

Ye didnay know he was there? said Rory.

I did not, no

She drinks in *The Rose & Crown*, I said.

What you talking about, you dont fucking know.

Och I've seen her a million times she works in Barclays Bank.

Does she fuck work in Barclays Bank she's a social worker.

Aye nowadays, but no then, no when I'm talking about, back in the old days

You dont know her.

I do sot, she's a Kerry woman – or is it Barra?

Bullshit.

A woman from the islands.

Kerry's an island!

The Kerry I'm talking about.

Crap.

Vik, I said, tell this guy.

You tell him.

I dont want to.

Tell him.

Bill grinned. Come on Colin.

It's lengthy.

We dont care if it's lengthy.

Mm, well, okay. Ye see there was this auld grandfather of mine, he was from the islands. I'm talking about the auld islands, way back before the forced dispersals. As a boy he not only went out with the herring-fishers he also went out with the what-d'ye-call-them, these birds that squirt ink at ye when ye try to save their fucking life, these yins that live down the face of these sheer rock cliffs. And then if they fall to the ground, kaput. Nay kidding, ye've got to pick them up and fling them into the air, poor wee fuckers, they cannay even fly off the ground, they need their ayn wee air eddies. And then when ye're trying to hold them without squashing them to death they turn round and squirt ink at ye, and ye're just trying to save their life tae, ye're trying to fling them to fuck man to safety! Know what I mean! They turn round and squirt ink at ye! Not only that but it's up to you to catch it.

What ye fucking on about? said Rory.

I'll tell ye what he's on about, said Vik. It was boys like Colin's auld grandfather that made the soup on these boats, for all the auld sailors. He had to catch the ink and cook it, it was the only available sustenance, that and fishheads and innards, then they crunched out the eyes, icicles hanging from their beards, they wrung them out and added pepper.

What?

Heh Colin, said Bill, you want to visit Hull.

Pardon?

Naw, honest, I'm telling ye, where the whalers come from, ye'll see it all down there.

All what?

That fishing stuff, especially if it's seals. Six boats a day, that's how many they had sailing out from there, once upon a time, and the women came down from Scotland.

The women came down from Scotland?

Yeh.

Ye mean ye didnay know that? said Rory.

Ah ha, I saw ye winking.

Naw but they followed the fleet, said Bill, a hunner years ago.

Honest?

Aye.

Rory said, Are ye telling us we've found something ye dont know?

Pardon?

We've found something ye dont know?

I beg pardon?

Ye didnay know that?

Sorry, I said, ye're losing me. I'm just no actually sure what ye mean, found something that I dont know, it's one of these dead tricky conundrums.

Ye didnay know what Bill fucking told ye, about Hull, about the fucking whaling.

Ah, right, I see.

Naw but ye'd appreciate it Colin, if ever ye're down that way I recommend a visit.

Thanks Bill, ye're a good guy, the same goes for St Kilda, if ever ye're up there.

Ye're a fucking cheeky bastard, said Rory.

See that Vik, he's got me dead to rights.

Vik yawned. It's no often ye need handers.

What ye saying, I need them now?

I'm saying fuck all.

We've aye been a team, revolutions or tangos, it takes two

and that's what we've been. No siree, I've never denied the need for handers, no potentially.

So he went to college with ye? said Rory to Vik.

He certainly did.

Worst days of wur life, I said, the dichotomy took off from the instant we entered the portals, I went in body and he went in soul. Even then it was only for a trial period, that was the saving grace.

But we gave it every chance.

So what did ye do when ye were there? said Rory.

Our theseses ye mean?

If ye like.

We presented them with the physicality of the One. Straightforward. In saying that it baffled the professors. Thus we became the men ye seeth todayeth, he was somewhere and I was somewhere.

Yeh, said Bill.

If he was in one spot then I was in the one next to it

If not the exact adjacent, said Vik. In fact that was the substance of wur theseses

Yeh . . . Bill nodded.

If I had got there before him, and if I was in front, and if the first and also the second, then he wasnay far behind. Is that a fair cop Colin?

It certainly is, one can say many things, very many things, very very many things.

Bill was nodding his head slowly. I see it . . . I see it all, what ye're talking about. Ye know when I was a boy, I used to hear my uncles and aunties talking about Elvis and the Beatles and the Stones and all that malarkey. And in some ways ye know I reckon that's how I got into sex, through rock and roll.

There's a talking point, I said.

So what like is it sleeping with a man? said Rory.

166

Ye asking me uniquely?

What else?

Well, okay, I take it ye must know it's sexual, that it would be the same thing with your brother, for him as well as me, that that would be sexual.

I've only got a sister.

And that that would be sexual too.

What, what would?

Sleeping with your sister.

What?

It would be sexual.

Naw it wouldnay.

Well it should be, naybody should shy away from experience.

What is he on about? said Rory. Apart from evading the point?

Belief, said Vik, that's what he's on about.

Belief?

Let me tell ye about belief, I said, I formed an opinion when I was a boy.

Did ye, well I dont want to hear it.

Bill chuckled. Dont listen to him Colin tales of childhood are always interesting, fire ahead.

Ah ye're the broth of the boy yerself now Billy boy listen and I'll tell ye: see there was a house across the back from me up where I lived in Drumchapel. Like Rome the Glasgow Council built it on seven hills, they've aye disguised the fact because it clues ye into their beelzebubian origins. Eh . . .

On with the story!

I've lost my fucking drift. Naw! Naw I huvnay. So, right, okay, in this house across the back from me there lived a family who were the enemies of mine – my family – they were the enemies of them. The two sides feuded, it went

on for years. I steered clear as best I could. A lot of people
prefer an easy life, I never have, which is not to say that myself
and suicide have been like peas in a pod. There's no need to
discuss self loathing, I found that out at an early age. But the
feud itself seemed childish, incredibly naive. And also boring
I have to say, even if it sounds like a criticism of my family.
So I steered clear, I let them get on with it.

Yeh? said Rory, yawning

Yeh, ye're a perceptive chap Rupert, considering ye take
nothing to do with politics, no offence, a lot of folk prefer
the easy life.

Rupert?

Rory, said Bill.

Rory, sorry. Yeh but ye're quite right, I said, fuck impro-
visation, the lust for perfection, and so on. If I was in the
painting and decorating game I'd be exactly the same. Like
I say, I was a great disappointment to my old man who was
a bit of a bigot, an Orangeman; whereas me, I rejected the
ideology appropriate to that particular prejudice. I just wasnt
interested. There was an additional factor, the wee boy of
the family we feuded with, I was in love with him, although
that came later. What is that post hoc procter quote from
the latin?

Post hoc procter, said Vik.

Spot on ya elitist bastard. Seriously but chaps, I was a classic
romeo and this was a classic romeo and juliet situation, given
our comparative youth, we were about 11 or 12 at the time.
His name was Billy as well by the way, so there's an unusual
coincidence. Life's full of coincidences for some folk. No for
me but, my life is different, there's scarcely a coincidence
from one day to the next, it's a constant exploration, a
navigation of never-before charted waters, a continuing trial
by mental ordeal.

Bill said, I know about Orangemen in the central belt of Scotland, I read the newspapers.

What newspapers?

Different ones.

Mm, ye've flummoxed me there. What was I saying again?

A boy ye loved, said Rory, a romeo and juliet situation.

Yeh, classical, except of course being only about 12 or 13 years of age at the time the pledging-the-troth bit was an unknown concept. Also, I'm embarrassed to say, it was an Eastern Star situation and that makes a difference, I dont know whether yous know that or not, being middle class, but after one of the reformations of the christian church matters of lust and nature were more outlawed than ever back home in dear old bonny Scotland, I'm talking about the calvinist workers, from wee boys to auld men, sexual innuendo reigned supreme and burnings were a commonplace, veritabilis.

I'm finding this unbearable, said Vik, it's gony end in scholastic philosophy.

Aw Vik.

Naw Colin it's time we were leaving.

What about the story? said Bill.

Fuck the story.

Ach Vik let him finish it.

Vik wants to get going, said Rory, he's tired.

There's time yet. Just till the soup appears. Finish yer story Colin.

You fucking love stories dont ye!

I do.

So do I. I think I was sent down to this world just to tell the damn bastards. What about yoursel?

I think I was sent down to make the damn soup.

What an ego! I said. What an ego!

Bill grinned.

How long is this soup gony be? said Vik.

Ten minutes.

Even I dont believe that one, I said.

There's still a drop of brandy.

A drop of brandy . . . ? said Vik.

Gie us yer glass.

Vik gave him it.

It's a pity ye've stopped playing music, said Rory.

He's not stopped playing music, I said, he's just stopped doing it for purposes of bread and pudding. Oftimes of an evening, when we're away on military manoeuvres, he takes out the old geetar and strums us a ditty. They're usually quite sad and melancholic, they remind the rest of us platoon-members about bygone times, when we were riding the range and the lonesome coyote was yowling.

Gie us a break.

Well we've all got to go. It's just for some of us we'd prefer it later rather than sooner, that's if we've got the option.

What? said Bill.

There he goes again! said Rory.

Mind you I'm not really caring, I just kid on I am, there's only so much a man can do and it's no more than his best.

He's spent his life lurching under severe burdens. Vik said,

That's the main reason he joined the armoured security industry, he got sick to death collecting waifs and strays. For a guy like him formalised forms of violence can be healthy.

Bill said, Is that right Colin?

If the circumstances are given.

Sounds like fucking fascism that.

It's just diplomacy. Everything ye think ye need as a

responsible moral unit remains that bit out of reach, never quite within hailing distance.

That's the beauty of it, said Vik, if ever you're looking for such factors, there's one of them. Take later this morning, us two, we'll be out there wielding the heavy weapon.

Exactimon, I said, and even to get to wur strategic onslaught we're forced to walk, the entire platoon of us, we're down to wur last coin. Mind you but that's the way we like it, armed struggle's got to pay for itself. Plus it's miles away so when one says walk, that's what one means, we cannay even hail a taxi. One of these fine days one'll find a field of action less than a stone's throw from one's place of domicility, but presently one always seem to do the exact opposite. I dont know how we manage it but we always do. So chaps, ye're definitely better leading your kind of life rather than ours because ours is open to question, I make no bones about it.

So we better make a start, said Vik.

Groan.

Your trouble is ye're half snazzled with the booze.

I aint half snazzled with no booze.

Ye're disgruntled but.

It's you that's disgruntled.

Let's move.

Naw, I'm damn cold. I'm damn cold and I'm damn hungry. And I'm fucking rooked. And the damn thread's bust on my damn fucking buckle, fucking bastard.

That happened on another continent.

So what?

The elements are there to be braved.

Naw they're no, that's sentimental shite. Plus Bill says the soup's coming.

They all say that.

Ah ye're a hard man.

Let him finish the story, said Bill.

Which fucking one! said Rory.

Christ he's a killer, I said.

The stories have to get told, said Bill, not just for our sake but for that of our children, and our children's children

Ye certainly do love stories Bill dont ye

I do, yeh.

I love stories as well, said Vik, I just demand the right to fall asleep now and again. The right not to listen, I demand that tae.

Where was I?

Fucking romeo and juliet! said Rory.

Ah.

I think it was one cold night in December, said Bill, the depth of deep midwinter.

Bleak bleak was the hour and chilled the tumbler. Vik yawned.

Yeh, yeh, it was the christmas party. And all the family had to wear dressing-up clothes. Maybe we didnay but I seem to remember we all had these paper hats on jees oh, and there was all these kinds of what-d'ye-call-them – french cakes – they had fancy icing on them, confectionery. The auld girl, my maw, she was a dab hand at the cake-baking. Whereas the auld man, he was the exact fucking opposite. But, paradoxically or not, he still insisted all us weans got involved in all these crazy social events.

Bill chuckled. I know the scene.

I think it eased his social conscience in regard to political activities Bill see he scabbed during a couple of strikes at the factory where he worked; he was known for it. That was what I had to put up with when I was a boy, having a known scab for an auld man. He had nay shame whatsoever. Never happier than when he was forcing us to enrol for some civic

172

cultural occasion, where we had to dress up in nice white clothes for a visiting member of the royal family, the upper echelons of the regional constabulary, whatever, that was his scene and he was neither proud nor ashamed of it. I mind at one christian sort of action forum we were all dressed up as wee supermen and robin hoods and florence nightingales. A whole team of us there weans; boys and girls, lads and lassies; maybe fifty of us, astonishingly bizarre. The lord provost of Glasgow was there as well, with his chains of state and full regalia, an ace socialist from the council labour party, on leave from the P2 order of the Knights of Columba. And they had this 70s music blasting out, that tuh twang tuh twang stuff that goes on forever and hardly ever changes; that kind of crappy sameness all the time

Yeh yeh . . . yeh . . . ! Bill laughed.

That's the music they liked and that's the music they played. In fact it was a need and their needs is another man's freedom

Rousseau's second principle, said Vik.

A twisted version granted but enacted nevertheless

Now ye're talking

Honest to god and I'm no kidding ye: *I Dont Have A Wooden Heart, Blue Rain in Acapulco, She Loves You Yeh Yeh Yeh, Stand By Your Man.*

That's 60s! said Rory.

60s yeh, what'd I say?

70s.

Yeh, 70s, so there ye are, the Eastern Star old fellow that's what I'm talking about, it was their christmas party. And when one looks back on it it was funny how come they were playing this kind of music, the crappiest music ye can imagine, birdy birdy cheep cheep or something, the kind of thing british politicians like to dance tae at the end of their annual conference, the one before god save the queen, or maybe it is god save the queen.

It depends, said Vik.

Us kids but we didnay know where to look, honest to jesus this was weird with a capital w. And it was gieing us a right showing up in front of the royal family as well, no to mention the chief of police christ almighty I mean we were expecting a protestant hymn if we couldnay get *The Sash*, and personally I was hoping for the dambusters' march like they play on the 12th in memory of whatever it is.

The death of the whales in the polar arctic, said Vik.

Right.

I think that was what the composer intended it for anyway, I'm talking about in the first place, when he sat down and wrote the original. It was just after that guy walked out the tent to do the honorourable thing.

The doctor, said Bill.

A never-forgotten moment, I said.

So there yez were all huddled together, said Rory. Eh? wee boys and lassies?

We certainly were, on massont, in wur wee red, white and pinky-blue costumery, blushing our wee faces off; and in some ways that's exactly it between these white rock singers and the impact they had on the music industry.

Fuck off.

Naw, honest, I'm no kidding ye, never mind the auld blues' players, the auld delta team, never mind them, that's what I'm saying ye're saying.

Get to fuck, said Rory.

It's as true as I'm standing here.

Naybody's saying that at all.

It sounds like it to me.

Bullshit, I mean if ye're gony fucking start eh . . . that kind of fucking eh . . .

Vik raised his glass. Slainte companero.

As true as ye're standing here, I said.

Slainte.

Shit, said Rory

What's up? said Bill.

I've only forgot what I was gony say.

Well keep trying, I said, it might be a nugget.

Yeh, you are a comedian.

Interesting ye should say that because my auld man had a habit of saying exactly the opposite, in many ways you remind me of him. Do you wear button-hole braces by the way, I know it's a personal question but one of the factors about personal questions is how so often when ye dismantle them, I mean bit by bit, what ye're left with – or rather, what ye might discover – re niggling factors, once ye examine what's left is, that on the whole folk are disappointing.

Aye, said Vik, but having said that it's a mistake to have high ideals, a grave mistake, dreamers and artistes are prone to that.

So they say, I said.

What about actors and musicians? said Rory.

Ye're no that naive.

You definitely are a cheeky chappy.

Cheeky chappy! Another example of how folk let personal issues highjack a dialogue. How come people dont just enter into the rationalist position, forget the subjective, let's talk and explore, begin from first principles. After all . . .

Vik said, It takes two to tangle.

Precisely.

Fucking bullshit.

Naw, said Bill, I know what Colin's talking about.

What . . . !

Back in the olden days . . . and not so long ago maybe, when it comes down to it . . . the christians, they had this incredible grip on the world . . . the parts of the world they had access to . . . it was an amazing time in the existence of humanity.

We were fucked for a thousand years, said Vik.

Fucked for a thousand years, I said.

The honest thinkers.

Good and true.

Good and true my boy good and true.

And we're still no out of it, said Bill, we're still unable to communicate without this breakdown happening . . . this lapse . . . it's a lapse

The irrationality of half-baked schemes and analogues, I said, metaphorical positions and a variety of animus, animi, neuter. Verily I say unto you, in order that we may not be moving, not be not moving.

Sit still and ye are dead, said Vik.

One's glass is now empty, said Bill.

That's what happens in this world.

Ye might want to stop for a five-minute rest but if ye do ye better watch it.

There's always these dirty bastards waiting to spring the trap.

What's a synonym for dirty bastard? I said.

Yeh . . . Bill nodded. Trust nobody . . . nobody . . .

Ye dont mean that? said Rory.

It's preemptive strikes my son, that's what we're talking about, you should know that better than anybody I mean to say that old fucker with the long black coat, he's round every corner, all set to cut swathes out yer ankles with that mammoth scythe he carries. That's how

176

ye're always better off taking transport if ye can afford it, public transport I'm talking about, less chance of waking up on a cloud.

Vik chuckled. Colin Colin Colin.

Rory said, How long ye known him Vik?

Who?

He's forgotten my name already, I said, that's what happens to intimate relationships. It's one of our only saving graces, as human beings I mean, it's the exact same thing when ye hang onto a joint.

Theoretically, said Vik.

Aye but theoretically's something.

What's up? said Bill.

Nothing, just the world, it's full of non sequiturs, and that wasnay one of them, as per fucking usual. Eh Vik?

Yea and verily I say unto you, non non sequitu, where in negation the second part of the statement bears not no relation to the first, yet in answering the second yea let the first be assumed as the case, even where this second part is left unsaid, as in the foregoing example which fits in with an emerging overall pattern, while at the same time the internal structure is becoming apparent, is becoming apparent, slowly and seepily . . .

Seepily? said Rory.

Indeedy do, I said, ye have to invent words if not concepts. And in that there exists an obvious coherence which ye dont often find in good craft or even honest art, although that's a prejudice on my part, given it's based on direct experience and that's always indisputable. My advice is find yerself a good woman and settle down; forget all this actors and musicians' malarkey.

Bill chuckled. It takes ye into bad company.

Bill, I said, let me grasp ye by the hand. Ye've had many a

position reinforced this night I'll warrant. But now it is time
we was elsewhere.

Ye not waiting for the soup?

The soup the soup the soup. Seize us yer hand. Let us shake.
Peace and security brother, pass the message onto yer mate; on
second thoughts I'll do it myself. Rory of the Two-Face.

Relax, said Vik, it's a translation from the Gaelic.

Here's my hand for an enjoyable evening.

You still looking for a battle matey?

Not at all. Let us shake off the coils and cobwebs of
infratricide, har har har, give me yer hand. Naw, seriously.

Aint he a one, said Vik.

Ye're a caution yerself mucker. Mind you it's a precarious
time for the armoured security industry, it's all yoicks and
tally-ho.

The profession's gone to the dogs.

I remember the good old days when continents were ten
a penny. Rory, are ye shaking hands with me? a forlorn
stranger, an itinerant peripatetic.

What ye talking about?

Just shake the guy's hand. Bill smiled.

Rory sighed but then he sniffed. Okay, he said.

On third thoughts, I said, smacking my hands together.
It's best not to shake. I'm talking about for the two of us,
our mutual self esteemaneighhhh.

Jesus fucking Christ!

Dont get angry, it's a test of will. Honest, I said, ye'll thank
me later. You coming Vik? I stepped to the door and opened
it fractionally. Beyond was cold, dark and scary.

Bill whispered, Bleak bleak is the hour, and chilled the
tumbler.

I thought it was a figment of the imagined murmuring.

Just breathe in, said Vik. Then set to with a will. Oxygenus.

Will you follow me? I said.

Of course.

I sighed then took a deep breath. Strange how that first step is always so damn fucking imposseebleh.

I know.

Bill said, Yez dont have to go.

Thanks, said Vik.

What about finishing yer story?

It wasnay a story, more a sad musing.

I guarantee the soup is coming.

We've had such guarantees before, said Vik.

Aint that the truth, I said and was about to add something further but the door creaked open, or seemed to. Vik shrugged and I glanced at the other two.

Some thoughts that morning

The subway was shaking the subway was shaking. Yes fine, fine. And we are all vibrating; amazing eh!

But surely there is just no question about the great swathes of hypocrisy lurking in the world? It is a central part of the entire whole and takes its existence from every last single solitary thing that belongs in the world, that is part of the world.

I seem to have known for a very long time that there is a certain point and so what, what the hell does it matter: nothing is as great as all that. Nothing. No one thing can ever be said to be the driving force. Of course that is one view and there are others. No matter what one is to make of them. But what do I know? Sometimes I feel like I am not really involved in 'the world' except perhaps by association, indirect association, therefore how can certain things be said? How can anything be said? What right do I have? I do not have the right. I have no right, no rights.

Yes the subway was shaking. The other passengers vibrating and not able to do a thing about it. So what? It was one of these shifts in the tracks that could give the illusion the driver had applied the braking system on the approach to the next station. But everybody knew the truth, they had travelled these tracks for so long; every bump and turn were members of the same family. Only a stranger to this section of the subway system would make a move to get to the exit at this moment, unless in a daydream, it might be done in an absentminded condition, then realising the mistake the

180

person would attempt some sort of ridiculous cover up, trying to make out they just preferred standing or some such nonsense.

How fantastic it all is.

At the same time it is reminiscent of being in a court of law. That is what life is like. The obligation to provide evidence, to substantiate yourself. That was the way I always felt anyway. Not that I was being forced. Except sometimes I felt like that. But nobody was actually doing the forcing. But what did that matter if this was how I felt: if I felt like I was being forced then I was being forced. If one is forced one is forced. Even though pretences are played out to the bitter end.

I was fed up with it. More than anything I was fed up with these questions, fed up with my voice, the sound of my voice banging round inside my head with all these questions. These sorts of perennial conundrums to do with the whys and the wherefores; yet who cares, no one cares. Why the hell should they?

It was incredible to think everybody might be like this. An entire world full of people going about having these thoughts. Billions of heads exploding. Their faces all calm on the outside while inside this utter turmoil.

Imploding is nearer the mark. This person in front. This particular individual who sat gazing out of the window into the darkness of the tunnel, the shadows. I could not quite see his face in the window. But I had seen it when I sat down. I could barely remember it except that it was so uniquely his own. At least such is the conventional wisdom. I was viewing the populace as a series of types. I felt like twisting right round in the seat to see him. He was of the owl-class, a set distinct but not wholly dissimilar from my own. I had seen these close types before and there were minor, crucial differences. If I had been a portrait painter that would have been fine,

I could have produced a large notepad and a charcoal and just said, Excuse me, and started sketching a few squiggles. I would not even have had to say 'excuse me'. Probably the guy would have accepted it quite the thing. With the advent of contemporary marketing techniques people are into the habit of having their space disrupted by strangers who are not really strangers except on an individual basis, they work for these conglomerates and corporations whose worth everyone takes for granted; said employees have defined requirements and job-tasks necessitating the use of ordinary everyday people so ordinary everyday people put up with it; they are used to it and as a rule do not feel threatened when these company folk descend on them with a folder full of private questions about their likes and dislikes as they pertain to the use of hair shampoo or bars of chocolate.

Or else a handheld camera: Excuse me, we're here to follow you about for the next hour and a half, just pretend we're not there and carry on with your business.

The right to remain private has been withdrawn. It is now taken for granted that subject-inviolability and the marketplace exist conceptually but must be up for challenge at a fundamental level, that such is the mark of aforementioned inviolability in respect of the subject nowadays, through a recent legislative manoeuvre on behalf of The Majesties courtesy of This House, moved through towards the end of the last parliament, unopposed by The Loyal Opposition, that henceforth subject may be deemed object insofar as citizens are a concern.

Thoughts like this made me smile because they were so up-front politically. If I said such a thing in my place of work people would look askance. I could say these things inside my head and frequently this is what I did, most particularly in crowded situations vis-à-vis the public transport system.

182

The powers-that-be are fuckpigs.

One of those fine days such a thought could be trapped in a new kind of internet, based on a form of pulse modulation. It wouldnt be too difficult.

Weighty topics.

For an instant I saw my reflection in the window. I looked good: better than fair to middling. I searched for a page of kitchen-roll I carried in my trouser pocket for emergency handkerchief purposes. It was all a pretence of course, my nose was as clean as the day is long. And the train made a singular shift in the tracks which signified we approached the next station. Sure enough the brakes were being applied, the couple of folk rising to win pole-position by the exit.

The need for a quick escape.

It was perfectly understandable. And also noticeable that parties heading the queue were both female. One might have expected the males to take the lead in their primeval role of competitive predator.

It was this being forced to find evidence all the time. Sooner or later it was guaranteed to send a body stark raving mad. And again that applied across the board. Billions of people are on the road to becoming lunatics. All because of that obligation to provide evidence. Why, in the name of all that is holy, should everybody feel so damn threatened. One looks for answers. One finds none.

People are exiting. Others are entering. One allows them their space. One sits gazing elsewhere, not forcing an undue self consciousness.

Bodies becoming uncertain of their day-to-day movements.

Being the cause of such a panic. Incredible the power of one individual, to force others into psychic turmoil; simply by looking somebody up and down, even while letting it be known that it – the look in question – is merely a look, performed unintentionally; wholly without malice and, on the available evidence, done in a wholly absentminded manner.

Yet still and all it would make no difference and might yet induce a panic.

These typical systems of power are so unfair. Unless one accepts that it is not a need. Yet what can be conjectured, if nothing else, is the fact that the individual person might care. But with other people sentimentality is always the risk. But why should any human being be forced to sit for whole stretches of time with their knees tightly closed as for example a woman wearing a dress. It was remotely imaginable. Not quite a nightmare so approximating to a horror story.

I had had a partner whom I did not love. Once upon a time we kept no secrets from ourselves. I had known that I did not love this partner. I questioned the notion itself and found it wanting. There was no doubt that many people loved. It had such currency it could not be doubted; if emotional facts existed in the physical world then love also existed. (Family is excluded from this equation.) But what then was I to do? In fact I knew what I had to do and that was 'nothing'. The act of doing nothing was okay, it was ample. There had been unthinkable thoughts. Certainly. Their very insubstantiality gave rise to nothing.

A woman could cross her legs. She crosses her legs and she risks further exposure. It is a risk she has to take. She is faced by such risks on a daily basis, in the company of visceral strangers, where unknowable threats are lurking. Yet what is a 'visceral' stranger?

These things occur.

The beauty of movement in the person who now sat next to me. This had been established once and for all by the entrance of other parties and their taking a seat next to her, causing her to move. The relaxed poise of that move. Perhaps she would have been more content had she been able to light a cigarette. There was no doubt she was a smoker. But what about me myself? I was a man that knew everything, right down to unknowable threats; a male at the ready, for all conceivable difficulties, e.g. some criminal-type holding up the train and waving a gun about. I would have it under control. I would have seen such reality as always possible, not imminent but possible. And I looked reasonably youthful perhaps identified as a young husband and father.

Across the aisle sat a couple in late middle-age; male and female. They had entered the carriage in conversation. They had continued this conversation. It seemed of genuine importance. It was to the exclusion of all else. Nothing the other passengers might do would ever concern them. Nor would it concern the woman seated next to me. But did it apply to myself? No, not at all, strictly speaking. These forms of self knowledge appear a wonderful thing that is the cause of great satisfaction, appearing beyond relief they result in temporary elation. I barely smiled. If I did smile it was perfunctory. Yet heightened, nervously taut.

The person next to me had become a linchpin.

This is also strange, that I could use a word and not know what it means in its literal usage, but such a word may yet provide the most apt way of describing what it is I can feel, something that is beyond dispute, beyond the merely felt. A fact of subjective experience. I can use a metaphor to get to it, because this is what 'linchpin' is, a metaphor for something I do not know what, not yet anyhow.

That must surely be described as positive. By this simple act of using language we take our own grip of the world. As we find it. But as of that moment I had – and always

185

have – to stop my knee knocking against the person seated next to me, stop myself letting this other knee knock against mine. Power circuits. Static currents. Physical relationships. The modulated pulses.

Of course the outcome would prove awkward. It ever was thus, and would remain thus. Life seems to preclude the immediate rise to the immediate occasion. Other bodies are only a further consideration. What should it matter what other people think, is a naive question. Yet it always arises. And what they did was their own affair; nothing to do with me nothing to do with them; the same as what I do is nobody's business, what a body does is not my business, and so on and so forth, round and round the rugged rock, disappearing into this circular tunnel, Hillhead east to Kelvinbridge.

I smiled, my thoughts pumping ahead. But it just was not good enough. Life: it dragged itself across one. It was not the other way about. Given His existence God did make things happen. Bodies firmly believed life was their own and they were so wrong. God's judgment was there. The unwillingness to accept reality, the God-given. It was the enormity of certain decisions appealed to me, and naturally a body should attempt to act fraudulently, to attempt the circumvention of the route, then discover a method of sustaining the blunder, even in the face of self knowledge. Yes there was a decision and yes, it was difficult: of course it was difficult; what else could such a decision be? Even when big decisions have to be made – difficult ones (and then when one made them) – it was just a case of finding the right way to go, it was there to be found and that was what happened, one found it, but it was there all the time. That was why people didnt like you for it. They knew the decision was there to be made and they didnt want you to find it because of the pressure it put on them; because it meant they should have been finding it.

186

This was a moment when anyone in their right mind should have been screaming in joy or for joy. A moment when at least I should have felt like it, whether I did or not. But the pressure was off me all the same. Even getting out of this subway, knowing where I had to go, I would just sidle by people, not looking into their eyes; I would gaze at the ground, a person who just gazes at the ground; I had done it before and would do it again, I could always do it again. There are these amazing escapes and we give them to each other, despite everything.

The wey it can turn

I wanted to go. I dont know why I was still there, how come I hadnay left an hour ago. It was weird the wey it happened. It could be fine one minute the next it was who knows, everything got twisted. There was something in her, like she had been hurt, and she wasnay gony let it happen again; that kind of stuff. Fair enough, but it wasnay me that hurt her. If she had just come out and said it, we could have talked. She didnay but. People dont like being vulnerable; fine, okay, that's their problem. I liked her as well christ she knew that, surely – how could she no know it, she must have known it. Hopeless.

Even being here in her room was a bit funny. The house was near the block of flats where my maw and da steyed. She didnay know because I hadnay telt her. I was hoping I wouldnay bump into my maw on her wey out to the shops or something. She was a nosey auld cunt, aye wanting to know what I was up to. The view here from Lillian's place was the same as theirs but no so vast cause it was low down in comparison. They were eleven storeys up. I used to like watching out the window for stuff when I was a boy, UFOs and all that crap. Ridiculous, except I never seem to grow out it. Daddy how big is the sky. These kind of stupidities. It looked like I was gony be stuck with them for the rest of my life. Funny the wey it went, how ye couldnay escape stuff. It could sometimes annoy ye; ye wanted to get away and ye couldnay. Imagine being here! Sometimes I thought about it. Christ.

188

Across the valley the light shifted again, the sun going down, all sorts of colours, fiery. I could still get these drowsy sort of childish notions, trying to figure out where the end of the sky was, the end from where I could see. I had it figured as Oban or someplace farther north. It would be great going for a hike up there. I went once as a boy and it was good, it was a good laugh, I was with the school so there was a team of us.

My fag was done; I stubbed it out on the outside window-sill, flicked it over the edge. Lillian was moving on the bed, changing her position. It flashed across my mind about her vagina, her body, under the bedclothes, but I got rid of the thought. It's funny how things belong to people. Even thinking about them, it's a thing no to do, ye feel as if ye cannay. I wanted to sit on the edge of the bed but it was out the question. At this moment it was anyway. No unless I covered myself up, shoved something on, my jeans. Maybe if I done that.

It was a case of keep yer nerve. Whatever she said that annoyed me the last time, I wasnay gony waste my head thinking about it. I couldnay remember what it was and wasnay gony try. Once ye get involved in that kind of stuff everything becomes significant. It's part of the problem. It doesnay matter what ye say either cause she's gony relate it, even if it's something that's away on a different subject altogether, she's gony get it to sound the same. It would have been oh so easy just to leave. That was how I felt. I could have done it nay bother. I saw myself walking down the road, out in the fresh air, getting big lungfuls, freedom. No looking back. Just so glad to be out there in the open. Maybe bumping into somebody and gon for a pint, sitting down and taking a sip of beer, right away from it all. It was funny. She enjoyed sex tae. She did. It was obvious. And all she had to do was look at me, she knew the effect she had. She got a smile on her face. That made me smile as well. We could get a laugh the gether me and her, that was a thing. With some women ye cannay, ye cannay even get talking, that's what ye feel. My brother's girlfriend was a bit like that. She talked all the time, that was all she done, bla bla bla. I wouldnay have minded it with Lillian, if she had been like that, it would've been awright, it wouldnay have bothered me, except sometimes ye felt maybe it was covering something up, folk that talk too much, there can be something no right about it. I felt that with the brother's girlfriend, the wey she went on and on. Lillian wasnay like that. What happened with her was this change that came on; snap yer fingers and that was that. I couldnay understand it. Things would be fine one minute then bam that was that, and ye felt like leaving. Just like now, that was the wey it was, amazing, events got so turned round. How could I even be thinking the wey I was? Ye dont notice either, no till it's happened.

She was lying on her side and I couldnay see her eyes but I knew she wasnay asleep. I crouched down next to the bed. She was facing in the way. Fancy a coffee? I said. She didnay move. I asked her again and this time her head moved a wee bit. Whether it was a yes or no I dont know but I pulled on my jeans and grabbed the cups, went ben the kitchen, threw the auld coffee down the sink.

I wasnay gony hand her the knife. I think that was what she was wanting, if she got me to leave, she wanted to force me into it. I wasnay gony but. If she wanted me to go she would have to tell me. Maybe it was a reaction. People dont like being vulnerable and relationships make them vulnerable. Ye get too close and they want to back off. I had that before with a lassie; we went the gether a while then she cooled down.

190

I liked her. Yvonne. My da and her got on good. My maw got on with her tae. They were expecting I was gony get married to her, all that stuff. My maw still talked about her, she thought we were gony get back the gether again.

Lillian was something else. I couldnay see my maw getting on with her. Lillian was too – I dont know – sharp, something, I dont know. The door opened and it gave me a fright. I was standing there at the sink waiting for the kettle to boil. It was this guy Martin. He had a room in the same flat and I had seen him before. It was obvious he was annoyed finding me there. He crashed about for a while. There was nay need for it. If he had a problem all he had to do was come out and tell me. I made space for him so he could get into the fridge. He went footering about on the bottom shelf. He kept side on, as if he didnay want me seeing where his grub was stashed. Four of them shared this flat and they each had their ayn wee hidey-holes, including Lillian. The guy brought out a pack of cheese, switched on the toaster-grill, got a couple of slices of bread and shoved them on the tray thing. I kept out his road. I was glad when the water boiled and I could get out.

It was getting dark, the quilt was up at her chin. I shut the door then went round and knelt beside her. She made a sound like she was coming out of sleep. I laid her cup down on the carpet and waited. Now she opened her eyes and there was water in them. There's yer coffee, I said. I knew she wouldnay have been crying or whatever, that wasnay how her eyes were watering. Ye were sleeping? I said.

She looked along to the dressing table, there was an alarm clock there. She had her tee-shirt on. She must have done it when I was out in the kitchen.

I waited for her to say something but she didnay. To hell with it, I took my coffee back to the window and got another fag. I heard her lying down again. I smoked the fag to the end,

191

just staring out the window, my mind wandering. I forgot all about where I was, everything. I got into thoughts of childhood, all sorts. I was glad about some stuff but other stuff naw. Ye aye regret things. Everybody does. That was how life went, some things worked out, other things didnay. I had made some stupit moves in my time. Nay doubt about it, stupit. I could see that now. Sometimes it was like I had the blinkers on and I couldnay see a thing and I would get these horrible feelings, about life itself, weird feelings, horrible, even the thought. Before I knew it I was back by the side of the bed, the jeans were off and I was squeezing in beside her again. She turned into me. It was a single bed and there wasnay much room. She hadnay touched her coffee. I lifted it for her and waited till she was sitting up before passing it. She switched on the bedside lamp, rubbed her eyes. I put my arm round her shoulder. A daft thought, I said, see if there was nay double beds I dont think there'd be any divorces. If it was just single beds, know what I mean, ye get too close.

She sipped at the coffee. That's how ye would get divorces.

Ye think so? I'm only talking about how people are forced to get close, close the gether, that's what I'm saying.

Mm.

Ye're forced to ye know I mean there isnay the slightest gap between ye; ye cannay get sitting but yer skin's actually touching, it's impossible for it no to be, that's how close ye get. It's crazy; cause then at the same time ye're supposed to act like ye're polite strangers, meeting on a bus or something. How can ye do it I mean what's the point, I dont understand it. I dont. Know what I mean, when ye think about it, we're as close as ye can get.

No we're not.

Aye we are.

We're not. It's sentimental.

Sentimental? What d'ye mean?

It is.

I dont know what ye mean.

Yes ye do.

I dont. I knew ye'd say something but, I knew that.

She smiled, shut her eyes. Then she opened them: Careful! One wee nudge and it was over me.

She was talking about the cup of coffee like I had been near to bumping her but I hadnay been, I wasnay even close to it, it was just an excuse. What does it matter. She inched away from me, holding the cup at arm's length. Ye filled it too full, she said.

I kept my mouth shut.

Ye did, she said.

It was right enough. If she had took milk it would have spilled. One problem was she didnay take milk so it was hard judging. She didnay take sugar either. There was a lot of stuff she didnay take. Diets and all that. She had a great figure tae I dont know how come she worried. She telt me she used to go swimming all the time. She had stopped it nowadays. I was wanting the two of us to start going the gether but so far it hadnay happened. Usually it was just the pub I saw her, then we came back here. It was a rut. No just that it was costly. I held my ayn cup out, leaning my head forward to take a sip. I took another sip, switched the cup into my left hand, put my right arm round her shoulders. She let me do it and her left tit nudged into the side of my chest; it was a good feeling. Even better if she took off her tee-shirt.

A thing about Lillian was how her skin was different from mine, smoother, if that's possible; the actual surface I'm talking about, it was a smoother texture. I was gony kiss her on the side of the forehead but I didnay, it was

193

too awkward. She was tense as well. It was difficult for her to relax. Ye were aye wanting to haud her, steady her, steady her down. A couple of times I said it to her, how she couldnay relax. I cannay mind what she said back. In a funny kind of wey I felt sorry for her. Although she was strong in other weys, she really was, so strong, it made me smile. Ye felt like kissing her. Stupit. Ye felt like it but. My hand was on the side of her arm above her elbow. I loved just feeling my fingers on her like that, her skin. I closed my eyes, feeling the twitches down below. When I opened them she was hauding her cup out again, balancing it. She gave her head a wee shake, she didnay smile but. Sorry, I said and got out the bed, a semi hardon and having to hide it. I went back to the window and pulled the chair across and sat down. So there it was, happened again. I couldnay believe it. I got the window open at the bottom, the draught coming in. That wey ye want to get the flu, I was glad to feel it, the cauld air, I felt angry. I wished to christ I was elsewhere, away someplace else altogether, I was sick of it, the whole thing. What was I doing with my life what was I doing? How come I was still involved in this kind of rubbish, cause that was what it was, rubbish, total rubbish, total load of rubbish.

As if I was gony bump her elbow. What was that all about? I wasnay anywhere near her elbow, I wasnay even close.

Christ.

These wee deals, ye cannay be bothered with it. I felt like gon for a pint. It's no as if I had money, a couple of bob just. No only that, I didnay want to. I was sick of it. The whole thing, it was a rut.

Now I saw her looking at me. It was her reflection in the window. She didnay know I could see her. She was looking right at me. I shut my eyes a minute then opened them. She was actually looking right at me, just actually looking, I

194

couldnay believe it. I shifted on the chair, making a point of seeing out. Down on the street I saw folk walking, some gon fast, the ones that were able to. There was a few auld people. Round from where my maw steyed was a sheltered-housing. Probably it was them. Although this time of the evening ye would expect them to be in the house, watching the telly or something, the fire on, drinking a cup of tea, recovering from their gravy dinner, potatoes and stew or something, cabbage and turnips. One auld boy had two walking sticks. An auld wummin was with him, a couple of yards ahead. Now she looked back. Probably she was worried in case he tripped and fell, would she be able to catch him. Shambling auld fucker. Probably a great fitba player when he was a kid. That was what happened, the auld injuries catching up with ye. What a nightmare. Even just reaching that age. My grannie and granpa on my maw's side were still alive. They lived out in Australia. People out there lived longer. My da was aye telling me to emigrate, that was what he would do if he was my age, bla bla bla. I could hardly remember what they looked like, my grannie and granpa. Terrible.

But this had been a good summer. It had. A lot of good things had happened. Except now it had passed. It would be winter the morrow morning. That was how it felt. See the autumn, when ye come to think about it, it hardly comes at all. If it does it only lasts about ten minutes then it's straight into the sleet and the snow, icy gales and showers, storms, and people having to scurry about the place like wee mice, hiding behind bricks. It depresses ye. Ye think of a place like the desert, how it would be there. Life goes on but wherever.

I went and got the remains of my coffee from the floor beside the bed. There was still half a cupful. I got my fags and lighter from the dressing-table while I was at it. I sat back on the chair at the window, about to light up. Lillian said, Men's bums are nice looking.

What?

They are.

Ye telt me afore they were too wee and round.

I've changed my mind.

Ye said they were like buttons.

They are like buttons. They're nice though, they're sweet, I like them.

Sweet . . . !

That's what they are.

Sweet?

Yeh.

It's a funny word to use.

Why?

It's no a word ye'd associate.

Why?

Men's bums ye know, sweet. Course you're a woman, I realise that.

I like women's bums as well.

I nodded. She gave a wee laugh. I knew it was a trap, whatever it was. She was looking right at me, at my back, no knowing I could watch her reflection in the window. I shifted the chair so we could see each other straight. All bums are nice, I said, the human body's nice.

She laughed again. God, ye really fancy yerself dont ye?

What . . . ? What d'ye mean?

Ye love to show off yer body.

Show off my body?

I'm no just talking about you. All men. Any excuse.

Ye're totally wrong.

Any excuse.

Ye're wrong, ye're totally wrong.

Am I?

Aye, christ, guys I know, they're no proud of their bodies. The exact opposite, if anything.

She smiled. It's any excuse.

Naw it's no.

Ye just love to show off yer body.

I dont.

Yes ye do.

Naw I dont.

Ye do.

I dont.

Yes ye do.

Naw I dont. But if I did anywey so what I mean is there something wrang with that? Eh? Know what I mean whit's wrang with it?

Nothing.

Good.

There's nothing wrong with it. It's like ye're children; it's nice – and ye're all so sensitive, that's the funny thing; at the same time as ye like to show off ye're all so sensitive; ye hate getting laughed at, if we poke fun at ye. Dont ye? Eh, dont ye?

What?

Ye hate getting laughed at. Ye hate it. Ye're so sensitive. You are anyway. I didnay realise it before. Ye are, ye're so sensitive, ye just cant take criticism at all.

What d'ye mean I cannay take criticism what're ye talking about? I cannay take criticism! Where did ye dig up that ane christ sake I've never heard that ane afore, cannay take criticism that's a beauty that.

I didnt realise it before.

Hoh!

I didnt; it's so obvious though I should've seen it.

197

Lillian I dont know what ye're talking about.

See what I mean!

Really, I dont.

She laughed.

I'll tell ye what I think but, I said, sometimes, just sometimes, what I think, women dont like men at all, that's what
I think, being honest, I'm no talking about all the time. It's
like ye want to get at us; it doesnay matter how.

Well it's the same with you.

Naw it's no.

Of course it is.

It isnay.

She smiled, shaking her head at me. Ye'll catch a cold, she
said, shut the window.

I'm okay.

It's a right draught coming through.

I was gony have a smoke.

Aw.

If that's okay . . .

Of course.

I know it's a no-smoking house. If ye'd prefer I didnay.
Eh? Would ye prefer if I didnay?

Smoke if ye like.

Is it an actual rule but?

What?

The no-smoking? I mean is it for the whole house?

Yeh.

Nobody smokes at all?

They're not supposed to.

In the whole house?

They're not supposed to. Not if they live here.

So it's only visitors?

It's not even supposed to be them.

198

Visitors arenay allowed to smoke?

Nobody at all, that's the rule.

So I'm the only ane?

You're the exception, yes.

That's amazing.

Why?

Naw, really, if it's rules, usually they're just for me, at least that's what it's like. See for instance when ye telt me I couldnay smoke in bed, I found that a real surprise. Honest, I thought ye had just made it up.

Smoking in bed's a rule for everybody.

Without fail?

Yeh.

How do ye check up? I mean if ye want to make sure naybody's doing it.

It's dangerous, and it's unhygienic.

Unhygienic, never heard that ane afore, unhygienic.

It is.

Unhygienic, that's a new yin. A new yin to me anyway.

And it's dangerous.

Dangerous okay, but no unhygienic.

Of course it's unhygienic, smoking? Smoking's unhygienic everywhere, it doesnt matter where ye are, if it's a bed or where ye are.

Up a mountain?

It's unhygienic, and it's dangerous.

Och I know, I know . . . I shifted back round on my chair again, seeing out the window. I took a fag out the packet. I hadnay even thought about it. I just did it without thinking. I sat there without lighting it. I tried no to see her reflection.

Are you okay? she said.

I'm fine. Fancy putting out the light?

199

She reached over and did it, then she got out the bed and put on her nightgown. Smoke if ye like, she said.

I'm no bothered.

Go ahead.

Honest, I'm no bothered.

It's okay.

I'll have one later.

I'm going to the bathroom.

I waited a minute eftir she went, then I lit up, blew the smoke out the window. But I only took a couple of drags, then nipped it and dived back into bed. I got comfortable. It would be good falling asleep before she came back. She was away ages, I was getting woozy. It occurred to me about Australia, if she ever thought about it, I wondered if she ever thought about it.

sustenance sustenance

My hands were pressing down on the kitchen counter. What was I doing? Trying to squash the damn thing! I felt angry rather than anguished. Why was that? Surely it was a case for anguish? Outside the wind whipped through the neighbour's washing. What a drying day! But I had missed it through indecision. It looked like rain it didnay look like rain. Much of the morning was spent working that one out and at the end it was a case of to hell with it I'll stick it up on the clothes horse. Near the window. It'll get the sun there. And that was what I did. But these vegetables. The carrots were well and truly finished and that had to be confessed. How come it always happened? And if it was so damn predictable how come people persisted in buying the buggars, me included? Then we persist in trying to cook them because they have a function and we have a duty to affix proper conditions, it isnt the carrots' fault, they do their best but have to rely on the human factor, so even when they are withering away into shrivelled little fucking whatevers – all soft and droopy – people are obliged to save what they can, we take such care in the preparation. But when it came to the grating process I always wound up grating my knuckles and these days my blood was a dark red, so that made matters worse. In fact my fucking blood it was like when I cut myself it came out congealed. And I seemed to be cutting myself all the damn time. Everywhere I went I was banging into things, crashing my knees on cupboards and door-jambs then that day I used the pair of pliers! they must have needed oiling they were so damn what's the word fucking whatever the fuck and when I closed them! Jesus christ almighty!

The leek was fine though that was one thing. Usually leeks do remain fine, there's always enough to use, ye can peel off the outer skins and eventually one by one ye get down to somewhere, to something, to some little fucking bit ye can always usually get some fucking little bit out it, out the thing. Even though it's all yellowed and soft ye can still make use of it for a pot of soup then too the same with onions. Thank god for onions. One can hear the cry. Slicing an onion is a relaxing occupation. Knives are correct for the job. The knife was correct for the job.

The leek, as a member of the onion family

But what about that garlic! People love garlic yet for me a let-down. These little efforts, they turn wrong too soon. I have no idea why that should be the case. Or have been the case. I tried leaving the half-full bulb on the kitchen counter next to the kettle so to remind me of its existence, like fresh ginger, of which there is nothing to be said. Then too the green chillies because I read somewhere the best thing of all is to wrap them in scraps of newspaper trying not to let them touch each other they hate even touching each other ye have to keep them separated after ye get them out the fucking polybag, ye look for a fucking sheet of fucking newspaper. Fucking unbelievable.

One needed a breath.

And of course one had to take one's hands away because there I was doing it adamngain and outside that wind blowing like fucking fuck knows what and the only time blood didnt come out was when I shaved, when I cut myself shaving, which was oh so rare these days anyway. So there was a thing that seemed to make a difference, the blood so congealed it couldnt even leave the damn cut. Ye imagine the people. Ye try to.

The Comfort

The phone went. It was Chic's wife. He telt me he was meeting you at seven o'clock, she said.

Aw right, aye.

Is he no there?

Naw, naw he's no here. No yet anyway. Being honest, I fell asleep on the chair. What I mean is he's maybe come but I slept through it.

Chic's wife didnay reply because she didnay believe me.

Oh there's somebody outside my door now, I said, if it's no him I'll call ye back.

Obviously there was naybody outside the door at all and this was me being roped into playing Chic's wife for an idiot. I dont like this kind of thing. Whatever Chic got up to was his business. If he wanted to be a lying cheating no-good bastard then that was down to him. I refused to enter into it. Now here I was being pushed.

I dont even know why I referred to him as my mate. Really, when ye think about it, he never acted like a mate at all. Contrary to what might be expected I have no time at all for these macho-bastards, the kind that run about chasing nooky – especially when they're 35 years old and married for nearly ten years. If he was wanting to act like he was 22 or something it was his problem. I knew he had been seeing other women because he telt me, usually under the pretext of wanting advice. I liked his wife. This was crap and I wanted nothing to do with it. Ye would have thought now he had a couple of weans he might have changed; not at all. When she went into hospital to give birth he was out clubbing it. I know cause I was with him. I think if he had walked in the door that minute I would have landed him one on the jaw. It was typical. The number of times he had fuckt me up never mind Linda.

I turned on the telly to keep my head clear.

Then I thought I would go out to the shop round the corner, get a breath of fresh air, pick up a few basics from the grocer. But the rain battered off the window. That meant changing the trousers, finding a pair of waterproof shoes, then the jacket, I didnay have a jacket, no a suitable one anyway. Thirty-four years of age and I was still without the proper clothes for my own climate, the weather of the land of my birth. There was a defect somewhere, definitely – in society at large or just in myself, no doubt in myself.

My father had been lord and master of the house from the age of 21 onwards, right until he took a stroke and started his carefree new life going nowhere and doing nothing.

Nay point blaming him.

Plus I had twenty years of mental alertness still to go, twenty years. Then I would pull the switch. I said all this to myself while pulling on my boots. There was this anorak thing I would use. I got it somewhere. It done the job, kept the wind out, but it hadnay been built for rainstorms on the west coast. Just as well I wasnay a fisherman, I would have died of exposure years ago.

There came another bang on the wall. The second time it had happened in the space of the evening. Maybe somebody was trying to tell me something. Maybe it was a warning. Maybe it was best no to leave the house. Under any circumstances. Maybe this was indeed a devilish evening, one that was best avoided. If the proud possessor of a warm fireside one was well advised to remain there heating the toes and keeping out the damn chill. Who the hell was the god of rainstorms? Some evil arsehole no doubt.

Fortunately I didnay have a warm fireside. I used to have one but when my partner got unattached so did the fire. The one I was using now is what they call a gas-miser; it was of indeterminate years. However, it fucking worked so no complaints.

It occurred to me that if I waited a couple of hours I could get the morrow morning's paper and maybe avoid the rainstorm. A sensible course of inactivity. Or else was I just a lazy bastard? Laziness had been the bane of my life. My mother defended me in the family home but it came to nothing, I was witnessed for the worthless article I was.

I was still deliberating when came a thud at the door. Bastard-features. I opened up and he came in without a word. I dont think he even looked in my direction. Chic, I said, what is it with you?

What?

Linda's just off the phone, she's worried and she's upset.

Aye I know. Any coffee?

Coffee doesnay solve problems, it causes them; the heart races and ye wind up in a false state of consciousness. You dont read enough, if ye read more ye'd know what I was talking about.

Give us peace.

Where's the half bottle?

What half bottle? He gave me a look that was resigned then fished it out his pocket.

Ye're turning me into an alcoholic, I said.

Me? I dont even like whisky.

Naw, ye dont, but so what, ye want out yer fucking head dont ye.

What's up with you?

Nothing's up with me. It's just got fuck all to do with anything but is it, what ye're talking about, whether ye like something or no, what does it fucking matter – ye aye come out with these stupid notions man it does my head in.

Chic stared at the gas-miser, then glanced at the half bottle. Are ye gony fucking open it? he said, What ye doing?

Look this is my house, what ye coming up here for and starting all this patter?

He shook his head, I saw his eyes were closed. I went ben the kitchen and plugged in the kettle, got a couple of glasses.

Pour, he said, pour.

I'm considering it.

Well fucking gie it to me then I've considered it already, that's how I bought the fucking thing, I considered it and then went in and done it.

That licensed grocer along the road, the one with the lassie with black hair and a saucy smile?

Shut the fuck up.

Cause you're spoilt for choice the rest of us arenay even supposed to think about it?

He stared at me pouring the whisky. I passed him a glass and raised my own: Here's to good grace.

He sat staring at the images on the tv screen, sniffed to cover up the fact he had sighed. I'm just gony have to fuck off, I'm gony have to leave.

How d'ye mean?

I'm gony have to leave, that's what I mean.

Ye mean Linda knows the score? But before he could answer there was a sudden loud crash of music from through the ceiling, fucking neighbours. Here we go again, I said

Go up and sort them out.

I canny, it's a boy.

Fucking sort him out.

Chic it's a boy, I'd get done for assault.

Well his fucking feyther then go and fucking tell the cunt.

His feyther's dead.

Chic sighed then started chawing on the edge of his thumbnail.

His maw works at night, he'll have a couple of his mates in.

Ye shouldnay have to put up with it. Can ye no tell the polis or something?

Aye, I'll go and lay a complaint.

Chic closed his eyes.

It's what happens when ye're single Chic, ye've got nay leverage; nayn of the local politicos give a fuck. No kidding ye, life just changes so dramatically, it becomes something ye've never experienced before – salute. I swallowed the whisky and glanced about for the bottle. Chic was waiting already. I refilled the glasses.

Let's go for a pint, he said.

D'ye want to?

Ach well I'm easy, if you dont want to . . .

Well maybe a thirst-quencher. Unless we got a couple of cans, we could get a couple of cans. Ye should've brought them man.

Fuck sake I'm no made of money.

Aye right, let's go then.

Whatever.

The music blasted after us all the way down the stair. Outside the close it actually got louder. The wee cunt had his window thrown up wide. When I stepped across the street I saw him and another boy up at the window, even with the rain lashing down they were sitting on the edge of the sill. Look at the silly wee cunts! I said, jesus christ they'll fall off!

It's no your problem Tommy forget it.

I'll have to fucking pick them up! So'll you.

No me. No you either if ye've any sense.

It's my neighbour's kids man they're part of the community.

Chic kept on walking, shoulders hunched into the wind, on round the corner. There were four pubs in the immediate vicinity but there were drawbacks to each; two of them just boring but the other two were no-go areas, sectarian disasters, prehistoric politics, the way ye asked for a pint left a mark on yer fucking forehead. And Chic was moving to enter the first yin, the nearest yin. What did it matter, I couldnay be bothered stopping him. He led the way to the bar. A cunt was lying on the pool table out-the-game, fucking comatose. It was a thing no to notice.

Two women were serving, one about 30 the other about 50. They were chatting and kept chatting till eventually the older one walked ower and Chic ordered the pints. There was a wee company at the end of the bar and one of the guys there was looking at me. Just curious. I recognised him. Maybe he knew me as a kind of local, seen me in the job-centre or the post office, maybe the betting shop. I thought about giving him a nod but I didnt, he wouldnt have returned it, and I would have been left there like a fucking idiot.

Chic said, Can I kip with ye the night?

I shrugged. The woman was waiting for the dough. We carried the pints to a table near the wall, no too far from the big telly. It was showing heavy-metal videos but they had nay relation to the music blaring out the jukebox which was old stuff or else maybe a tape belonging to one of the women behind the bar. Billy Crystal and that kind of thing. See I cannay face going home, he said, I wouldnay ask except . . .

Ye are asking but.

I wouldnay if it wasnay important.

I'm no into deception Chic I cannay handle it. If Linda knows where ye are fine, if not . . . Fuck me Chic I'm no into it, that's all, okay?

He was silent.

I had it myself man ye know I cannay handle it, I cannay.

What ye saying then?

Nothing, I'm no saying nothing.

Then he muttered something, I'm no sure what, it sounded the kind of thing Chic would never say. Sometimes ye hear things ye think somebody's said whereas in reality it's a thought of yer own, and lately that kind of thought had been part of my own consciousness. I would be watching the telly or listening to music and I would hear a comment and either I had said it out loud or else I had thought it in a strong clear kind of way so that it came like somebody else had said it and I would catch myself looking to find who it was. I had been on my own too long. I had more or less stopped reading. I thought when I sold the computer I would have got back into it but I hadnay managed it yet, it was like I was building my concentration towards it, I tried to get down the library once a week, hoping to get myself the habit.

I saw Chic staring at the game of pool. One of the barwomen came out and shook the guy out of sleep and another two guys came and dragged him off and dumped him on a chair, then paid the cash and started racking the balls.

One of them was quite good – blootered, but holding himself the gether, playing it dead slow and measured, relying on direction and safety, doing nothing with the cueball, he

210

wasnay even crouching. Then once he played a shot he turned to the spectators for applause, taking a bow. The other guy was a batterer, end of story, but he was managing to hide the pockets in all sorts of flukey ways.

I didnay recognise them but that went for nothing, it was only once in a blue moon I came in. Evil things happened from here, as far as I heard, ye had to go cautious.

Three women were sitting at a table behind us and I was making it clear we hadnay noticed them. One of them was nice. I had seen her before. I think she worked locally, maybe at the Asda.

Some crazy bastard came lurching out the pisshouse and he went staggering across the floor, and then was standing at the head of the pool table with his hands deep in his pockets like he was finding money to plonk down on the table. He was out his fucking skull. An auld guy with cropped white hair, the build of a bent skelf, this caved-in chest. His eyes were shut and he was swaying. He didnay have the power of speech. It reminded me how when ye were really far gone on the booze yer IQ dropped, ye regressed. This guy looked like he had gone down to about 60, whatever he had been to begin with. The older barwoman was shouting at him that he wasnay to get playing and no even to consider the possibility. It wasnay penetrating. He just swayed there, his brains trying to make sense of the phenomena in front of his eyes. He really was in a bad way but and that was one of the things about this fucking dump man how they let a guy like that get a drink, it was fucking out of order. One of the pool players passed to play a shot and the draught made the auld guy stagger back, his body picking up speed. He came to rest against a pillar. His legs went limp from the shins up through his knees but he was staying upright. It would have been funny except it was sad. He had on a pair of joggers and one of these vests that show off yer biceps but he was so fucking skinny the joggers needed braces.

The younger barwoman came out and round to the side behind where we were sitting, I heard her joining the talk with the three women. She was definitely some bit of stuff. I had noticed the last time I was in. I got up to go to the bar in a roundabout way, hoping the barmaid would see me from behind. Then I saw her looking up but it was at Chic. She did it in such a way she might just have been staring and not seeing anything, but I knew the signs. Chic hadnay noticed, he was getting out his seat. Then he was laying coins on the pool table, and walking towards the gents. I couldnay believe it, after what I had telt him. The older woman served me the drink. When he came back I said, Chic I fucking telt ye man ye've got to go careful in this place.

Ach.

I'm no kidding.

You playing?

Naw, they're fucking mental cases man ye've got to watch it.

Ah well I'm past 21.

The smash of the balls and the next game was underway. We're gon hame eftir this pint anyway, I said.

Are we?

Aye.

Suddenly ye're fucking angry.

I'm no angry.

Ye look like it to me.

Is that right.

Aye.

Well just fucking screw the nut then.

He sniffed, rocked back in his chair, his feet coming up to settle his weight against the spar under the table. The barmaid

212

from behind us reappeared when a couple of new customers entered. Chic said, She's a darling int she.

Think so?

Tommy . . .

What?

Gie us a break?

Ye're asking me to gie ye a break, I said, but ye'll no tell me what the score is; the way I'm looking man you've got the fucking deathwish.

Who played that?

He was talking about a song on the jukebox. I didnay answer him. I didnay even know apart from it was something out the charts. If I had known I wouldnay have telt him. Look, I said, ye've fuckt Linda about before.

Chic stared at me.

Well ye have.

Have I?

Fuck you.

Tommy ye know nothing. And when it comes to women ye know even less. Fucking married for fucking ten minutes and ye've got the cheek to talk to me!

What?

What, aye, what.

So it's us that's fighting?

Are we?

It's in your fucking hands innit.

Ah well aye, fine, when it comes to decisions, nothing much fucking changes does it. Chic shook his head.

What ye talking about?

He sipped at his beer and studied the poolgame. I saw the barmaid glance at him again. It was beyond me about women. It really was. She was actually interested in him. He didnay wear a ring but even if he had what fucking difference would

213

it have made. What did it matter the whole carry on, marriage vows and all that keech. You're next on, I said, go and fucking play, get yer fucking heid kicked in. And dont fucking talk to me about fucking cheating, I said, just dont fucking talk to me about it.

Tommy, shut up.

I mean what the fuck did we come here for? I telt ye it was a fucking honkytonk.

How long we been mates?

We arenay mates man dont give us it. Ye keep dropping me in the fucking shite know what I mean ye didnay even let me know Linda was gony phone. So I wind up looking like a cunt. She knew I was at the fucking fanny. She knew it, when I was talking to her

Chic shook his head. I stared back at him. Then he said: When did ye last shave? Eh? Ye grumble about women all the time man but when d'ye ever do anything about it, ye dont even try, look at the fucking state of ye. Christ, who's gony look at ye twice, nay woman's gony look at ye twice, look at ye! Naw, nay kidding ye man ye've let yerself go. Honest. I mean ye split frae her fucking five year ago, know what I mean, when did ye last have yer hole? Fuck sake, shouting about me and Linda, ye dont know fuck all about me and Linda.

He shook his head again and got up from the chair, left his pint on the table. I watched him get the coins in the slot, pick up a cue. He looked back at me and shook his head. The guy that had won the last game said, Me and you mate?

Aye, said Chic.

I sipped at my pint. He was blaming me for something, I saw how his hands were shaking when he played his shot.

It was strange how it happened, how things happen.

I sat there with the pint in my hand and when him and

the other guy moved round the table I felt like I was on a different planet, neither one of them entered my mind. And the guys at the bar, the women at the table behind me, it was like a cushion of air between us. The only thing in my head was the idea of getting myself home, no so much in one piece but just to get home. I wondered how long it would take me to make the move; there was also a roaring sound in my ear, a surging noise. Now I felt like I could start crying, something, maybe if I blinked; then too wee things, the laundry. Maybe I wouldnay make it. Maybe I would just collapse, get hit by a bus when I crossed the road; what were the things? There was that much.

Having another pint?

Chic was standing there.

I'm no that bad, I said and when I looked up at him I saw that worry on his face, it was so fucking horrible, I just wanted to pat him, pat him on the shoulder and I felt this hole in my belly, looking at him again, like his head was gony turn out to be a skull. Chic, I said, fuck sake man.

Into the Rhythm

Then the next night I jammed myself into a ticket collector's box at the gate entrance to a travelling funfair. It was good and tight and I could wedge myself in and get a good sleep standing up. It was great. I wasnay getting much sleep, I wasnay getting much of anything at all through no fault of anybody's except the political system which had it as the highpoint of civilisation for folk like myself that liked to ramble, that selfsame political system. Except this amazing hole had appeared in my left shoe, at the most unusual spot, not where pressure comes but who knows, it was like a spear had been thrust through it and I got the funny feeling it was these fucking MI5 bastards up to their no-good surveillance carry-on. How in the name of Christ they figured me for a danger I dont know but there was too much evidence these days, I had to take it seriously. I was born around that difficult period they had, coming out the dark and dingy strife-ridden sixties. There was a whole generation of us being tracked down. It was like that tale from the old testament, the pharoahs were set to wipe us all out, the entire kit and caboodle, right from the face of the earth, the last of the political thinkers. So I got off my mark. No sirree thank you very much. My plan was to walk away. I had heard tell of a wee side tunnel under the English Channel, apparently a wee group of syndico-workies decided to lay it unbeknownst to the powers-that-be, at the same time they were building the chunnel proper. That's how come it took so long to build. What a fantasy!

216

There's problems rambling but many of which are severe.
If ye think ought of severity then this is the life for you.
When I woke up I kept repeating to myself Christ sake, a
real sleep! This is what I was saying walking down the road,
Christ sake, a real sleep! It doesnt matter what they do, oh
no, they cant take that away from me – a song my old man
used to sing when he took the bi-monthly dip in the enamel
jug we laughingly called a bath. Mind you he was a wee cunt
so it was a snug fit and the conditions for future descendants
were imparted genetically. This is why I could spot sleeping
spots like the ticket collector's box at a hundred paces in the
surefire knowledge all else would fail.

It was also why the family would end with myself. I took
the necessary step last year. Henceforth I could screw forever
and impregnation would not transpire. Most women I knew
would enjoy the knowledge, they really would, being the
kind of guy not frowned upon by the gentler sex.

A tap supplied water at a nearby latrine. I rinsed my
mouth out with it but didnay chance swallowing the stuff
because although it looked fine it's difficult to tell with
water until afterwards. Okay it might look brown and that
puts one off but then somebody comes along and tells
you this brackeny stuff is the finest water in the entire
kingdom of united soveriegnities. This particular sovreignity
(I cannay even fucking spell the word man) wherein I found
myself was small, less than a million people lived there
but they were all nice to know and didnt represent any
threat. The citizens all thought they were well-off. And so
they were.

I needed a lift though because there I was, a crisp pre-dawn.
If I failed to get a lift I could walk down the coast and on down
to a certain large town. There was a bridge there. I couldnt
remember if I would have to travel through a certain other

town. Maybe I would just stop off at one or both, and chase the luck.

I tried this yesterday, kept walking for ages, away out the wrong side of town, so way off the mark that I noticed I had reached a farm for Christ sake. Fortunately there was a big boulder at the side of the road. I sat down and took off the shoes, wee bits of newspaper were giving me bother, the poor old soles were disintegrating because of that bastarn hole that got pierced. I fingered it and the dirt out, gave the toes a good-going massage. This effected a suppleness I thought had gone forever. Then suddenly I was tired again. Sleep will come when the body tires, when the mind is slack, at the beck of the physical. That was the way I was. So I went to sleep there and then but as usual the sleep was troubled. I was so fucking knackered tae and I'm talking about when I woke up. Fortunately I still had a biscuit from a previous life. Naw but seriously, a few nights back I got into an estate-agent's office and found thirty-eight pounds and sixty-two pence, a packet of biscuits, a jar of coffee and a jar of tea bags which looked like it had been a jam jar and then somebody thought to themself, this is an ideal jar for stashing the tea bags, and had rinsed it out then dried it all for the purpose. The day after that I got a good-going meal, bought and paid for. This was the day before yesterday. The first place I went to the waiter said there were no tables for single persons. He was embarrassed. I made it easy for him, an undemonstrative exit. The second place was fine. How much did I pay for that meal? I cannot remember. It was good though. It was chinese. The table where I was put had a red candle. At the time I thought it was quite special but it might not have been, it might have been an average thing, that kind of experience.

So I got through that day and this day okay and then the ticket collector's box was the veritable cake-icing and now

look at me. I was still sitting on that boulder when a car
stopped at the merest flicker of my eyebrow such that I had
to discard my suspicions as to his motives, else why had he
observed me so minutely as to pick out that eyebrow twitch.
I thanked him but for stopping, a guy about fifty years of
age, give or take a decade. No trouble, he said, no trouble.
Where you off to or are you just drifting, not that it matters
to me in fact I've often thought of it myself, commitments
commitments eh though never mind I've got to admire you
in a way though I suppose rejecting society and wanting to
lead your own life, well, as long as you dont interfere with
others then they dont interfere with you, that's what I've
always said. London? well cant have you walking all the way
now can we. No, they dont interfere with you, who's to say,
you got to come and go in this world otherwise what's life all
about, I often wonder at these people who go about and do all
the talking but when it comes to getting out there oh no, not
them, you dont see them for dust, it's a different kettle of fish,
I was in there in town seeing this fellow in regard to spring
holiday orders and they've still got their summer ones to come
and I thought to myself well you lucky devil, when you look
at some who spend all the year, they do, they spend the whole
year long and then when the time comes they cant afford a
weekend in Margate, now that's what I call irresponsible, I
dont know about you, if they have a family, that's what I'm
talking about, they've got their priorities all wrong, if you ask
me. I cant afford to go around with my eyes closed, no, cant
afford to, and it doesnt bother me if Mister such and such is
on sixty times the salary I'm on, not if it's fair, if it's fair then
what do I have to complain about, I'm not going to grumble
about it now am I, but take yourself, in your situation, what
happens when you hit middle age, generally speaking guys
like you, sticking to your own ideals and principles

219

Poor fucker.

Maybe he wasnay.

No matter, I was settled back in the nice comfy upholstery, gazing at the nice country road ahead, thinking to myself a thousand quid would be nice. Yeh. Even a hundred. One job I worked I won the pools. I was a boy at the time. My journeyman pestered me into putting a line on his coupon and I did and I got 7 score-draws but it was a poor pay-out and it only threw me £5.70. That was the last occasion. Prior to the cheque's arrival I spent countless hours figuring my future: was it to be India or South Americay, and would I buy a young foal on spec, a future great racehorse, champion in embryo, or would I go for one that had already won a couple of races, maybe buy it out a good class seller, wait for a York meeting. What an eye for a horse I would have once the dough was available. I wouldnay even spend a hunner thousand, would I fuck man no even a fifth of that. I would be walking down a lane in a despotic tyranny similar to this yin and I would see a young nag chewing grass in a dowdy field, a sparky little thing, whinnying away at its mother's underbelly, eager for fun and games, smitten immediately I would make the owner an offer he couldnay refuse, then being introduced down the *Dog and Duck* tavern, the farmer's local: this is the very young lad who bought the little chestnut foal, such would he tell the other worthies, all stable-lads and ex-jockeys. A year and a half later I would have won the fucking Gimcrack and then what? the Derby or the Arc, that big race in Japan, or else the fucking Breeder's Cup man who knows it's all up for grabs these days, Dubai man wherever.

Then the cheque arrived from the football pools company.

Well well well, fuck all.

But I didnt complain, it being naybody's fault. There were

too many winners that Saturday. It seemed like everybody in this entire kingdom of aristocrats and upper crustaceans got a return for their meagre investment. So why sulk? But never again never again. Even although my workmate had already advised me about the probability of a poor pay-out I was still in a deathlike state. I had refused to listen, given he had based his opinion on long years' experience. I preferred to discount these long years' experience, insist upon my dream my dream my dream, fuck it.

The driver had been silent for some time, the guy that had picked me up, the so-called travelling salesperson. Now he said, Look at the mist, isnt it spooky?

Yeh, it was spooky. It reminded me of these movies where flirtatious ladies in tight bodices keek out from behind trees, tempting one on into unimaginable horrors, old Vincent Price creeping out from behind a large bush, an evil glint in his eye, and the broken cross on the cemetery hill, the shadowy head of the wolf baying at the moon. Then it reminded me of the lassie

what lassie?

just the lassie. She was valid even if the dream wasnt. What dream was that? It was a sort of daydream, I had set it into motion myself, yestreen, no moonlight but millions of fucking stars.

How does that happen? How can one see all these stars yet there is no light from the silvery moon.

But this mist, the one I was talking about, often it heralds a bright new morning, even for travellers, the heat meeting the cool, from the ocean in the way or the land out the way. In these old horror movies, if it wasnt the studios down in London and they actually filmed it in the countryside then it would have to be the summer, so therefore the mist was that great dissipating thing, the curtain

221

being drawn and here we have sweet buttercups amid the morning dew.

I was out the travelling salesperson's car by this time, in fact I had got out it a while ago. Nothing against the guy, he didnt even depress me, I just felt like getting out for a walk, a bit of space. Plus these daydreams can drive a body nuts. I wasnt in the mood for that, I had another thing on my mind, I was thinking about it now, running demented zigzags round me, whatever it was, some numerical fucking concept, a brainwave, cast-iron fucking laid-on certainty to make dough.

I couldnt drag myself out it, each moment I sailed off into my head it was there, how could it lose how could it lose, it was to do with how they would fall, numbers, numbers were gony fall, they would fall, and what my exact next move would be then I thought oho who the fuck knows, life, what a treat, yes, might have fucking known, it's these fucking machines again, them I played when I was a kid, thirteen/fourteen, I was never done playing them, went to bed dreaming about them, machines.

My auld man wasnay a bad singer really, when ye come to think about it. Everywhere he went he sang. The likes of that driver guy, my da would have sang a song at him, a big cheesey grin on his face, maybe holding the guy's wrist, that was what he done, the auld man, fuck sake, he held yer wrist and sang a song at ye till after a while ye stopped squirming, ye felt yerself relax, that was how ye found yerself, he forced ye to relax. My maw used to look into his eyes, ye knew she loved him but it made me and my sister feel weird.

So there ye are.

The mist still hung about.

Even so.

But then that lassie Josie, how come she was filling my

head, I had met her a few days ago at the bus station and she told me there was a good pub and I should go there, her and a mate would show up later. Naw they didnay. I sat for two hours then counted the dosh. Trouble ahead. I figured on a walk to spin it out, maybe I would meet up with a generous stranger. Out I went then back to the pub. I must have been taken with this Josie because I still had it in my mind she would show. Probably it was her name. But that was me now, I spent the tank waiting. Late on the bartenders were upturning chairs onto tables. One of them said, If it was up to me you could kip under the counter, sorry mate. He smiled at me; there was no sarcasm.

Outside the rain was drizzling, of course. Best heading for the outskirts, find a bit of safe shelter.

It was more like a big village, unless one happens to be a farmer. I passed the entrance to a club not far from a small shopping centre. *Mr Parkes* it was called and promised much revelry.

The doormen just looked at me. I walked away. But I doubled back and round behind the club I found three big bins down the lane. One of them had a pile of newspapers, all with the same date; there was a heat from them, I put my hand down the middle. The rain went off later. I hoofed it along the out-of-town road. There was a bowling green. The gate was open. Inside was a sturdy little clubhouse with many windows. The lights were glowing and I could see figures at the bar, not many, like it was closing for the night. I walked past the windows and at the far end was a couple of tennis courts. I found a bench beside some trees and sat down on some newspapers for a long while, elbows on the knees and that kind of thing. I was not down, not at all, it was just a general kind of low depression, I was a part of it; that was about it really.

At some point the clubhouse door was getting locked, voices rising and falling, the clank of the gate, then me, just me. I wondered whether I could sit there and just whatever, remain. A breeze rustling the branches.

I nudged at the gravel with my shoes, cleared a wee space. There was nothing in particular – except the idea of course, there was that, some idea. What the fuck was the idea? I cannot remember. I cannot even remember, what the idea was.

But I had about three weeks left. This was at the very most. Otherwise I would be as well giving it up entirely. But I couldnt renege on it, that idea, whatever it was; I just couldnt, it was out the question.

Fuck. What else?

The wind came from somewhere and lifted dust from the tennis courts, all over me, I was picking it out my hair. I could imagine myself getting a fit of the giggles, at some other time, some far off occasion. Ach but fuck sake things would be better in the morning. But it took ages to arrive, much longer than one might have anticipated, if one was in an anticipatory frame of consciousness. I dont know if I was looking for signs. But the gap between dark and dawn went on and on and on, and I was having to change position the whole night, my hipbones, feeling like they were red-raw. I thought about stretching my legs, getting myself up from the bench, going for wee walks about the place. It was getting to rabbit-time, if I could find a rabbit, I could kill a rabbit. And the freedom would not come. Or was I dreaming, maybe I was dreaming, hearing that song in my nut

Josie, I wont fail you
I wont fail you

Strength

I asked her what she was thinking. She told me she was thinking about that night I had the brainwave. It wasnay something I wanted to talk about but the way she caught me I did it without meaning to. That's right hen, I said, it was late on and I had turned off the fire and the lights and all that, you were away to bed, I just sat down with the paper for a minute.

Ye pulled out the plugs.

Well aye, I always pull out the plugs.

I heard ye through the wall. Yer memory was playing tricks.

It was playing tricks, that's right.

Ye told me that.

Well that's right, aye, it was.

Ye were back with that wee lassie on the pillion of yer motorbike. You and that motorbike. You loved that motorbike.

I just told ye because I thought ye would want to hear.

It was a brainwave, that was what ye called it.

Well aye, I didnay know what else to call it, it just came frae nothing, I telt ye that at the time.

I like hearing things when ye tell me, even when I dont know ye're doing it. Ye had the lassie on the pillion and ye were on yer motorbike driving down to a pub in Gourock where yer friends went, away past the Dumbarton Rock and the tide was out and ye were thinking about Mary Queen of Scots incarcerated there in the dungeon, ye were going to the nightschool and doing yer exams, and ye came crashing down. Ye were seventeen.

I was, that's right; too young for the pub, we used to creep in and my pal got me a half pint.

No for the first time.

No for the first time naw, I had a couple of crashes.

But that was the worst.

Aye, aye it was the worst, by far, the lassie broke her pelvis, wee Joannie, I suffered the leg break, it took months to get better. I missed that exam as well, the nightschool it was.

The policemen says ye were oh so lucky no to be lying there dead on the side of the road, silly young buggars. That was what they says to ye; silly young buggars. But ye were, the two of ye; you as well as her, ye were silly young buggars.

She was shaking her head at me now but I saw her smile, then she turned back to the television.

We were lucky to escape, I said. But she wasnay hearing me and I stood up and crossed the carpet, I took her hand and held it. We were lucky to escape, I said, we were lucky no to get killed. If I had I wouldnay have met you.

She shifted one foot up onto the pouffe. This was the way she sat but the pouffe was too high off the ground and it meant the foot was higher than the knee and that was bad for circulation, her leg stiffened up and it made her back worse, it was a grumbling condition and it must have been hard for her; I wouldnay have coped with it myself. There's nothing worse, ye try and forget about it but ye cannay, it's just always there, every time ye move, even if ye dont move.

You were elated, she said. That's what ye were, ye says that to me.

I was elated, it was a great thing about the bike.

That was what ye says to me, ye felt so very close to yer wee lassie and ye were elated.

226

I was, aye, but just being on the bike, it was a great feeling, it's hard to describe.

Hh, she smiled again, I only wish she had gave ye more sex because I know ye need it. I think she thinks that too, I do. Ye says ye were angry at her mother for letting her think it was something to be doled out once in a blue moon. That was what ye says.

Aye but I was only kidding.

Ye says that.

Aye but I was only kidding hen I was kidding ye on; I didnay mean it like that really; it's just patter, I was just saying that to ye.

Ye were angry at her mother.

I wasnay angry at her mother, I was just kidding ye on when I says that.

She told the wee lassie a pack of lies.

I wouldnay have says that, a pack of lies.

She filled her head with nonsense, that was what ye says. She told the wee lassie a pack of lies; what she filled her head with, her mother, that was how ye were angry at her.

Hen it's daft talking like this.

I dont like hearing how the two of ye drifted apart, no for anything special, probably just a natural progression ye says the way life goes. The habits ye had were aye bad for ye but ye never changed them. I know ye loved that wee lassie, but it doesnay bother me. Even if ye had got killed the gether, the two of ye, it still wouldnay bother me. I just admire ye both, I do.

She looked round at me and she nodded her head. I do, she said.

Her cup was on the carpet at her feet and one of her slippers was falling off. Her back would get sore as well with her no sitting right. I pulled the slipper back up. Ye

227

see that, I said, it's no my bad habits it's yours, these sore backs ye get, it's nay wonder, they're to do with how ye sit and stand and how ye hold yerself when ye walk. If people dont have the proper posture they rue the day, ye know that. It even includes sitting down, if ye've got yer feet up, it can cause pressure on the spine. Honestly hen I mean it, I'm no just saying it it's true, ye've got to sit right.

She shook her head, still smiling. Even if ye had got killed the gether, the two of yez, it still wouldnay bother me.

It's nonsense talking like that.

It wouldnay bother me, it wouldnay.

Ye're just worrying about nothing.

I would still admire ye.

Honestly hen it's nay good when ye talk like this, I hate it, I dont like it at all, and it's worry about nothing, that's the thing about it. It is. Ye're just worrying about nothing. It's all auld stuff as well, it's finished and done with, so I dont know what ye're goin on about it for. Is that no right? Do ye no think that's right? When ye let these auld things go through yer head, it's daft, it's just getting raked up for nothing.

Ye were too young, no ready to get serious. I blame her mother, I do.

Och it's aw past.

What I think, I was thinking about it, it would have to have been for keeps because ye both recognised something in each other that was strong and ye hadnay seen it afore and neither had she and it made ye scared, the two of ye, ye were too young, no ready to get serious, settling down, but my sister was only seventeen, virgins except with each other, her and Harry, ye could wish everybody would be the same about it only they arent, some are more advanced than others. They are.

Aye but it depends what ye mean hen, it depends.

228

Ye've got these big fingers, but they're clean and yer nails are neat and tidy.

I just done the dishes.

Ye always kept yerself neat and tidy.

Aye, I have, aye. You liked it but, you liked it about me. Ye telt me to my face, ye liked it. Ye did though, that was what ye says to me. Aw but you were aye stubborn! Ye were. Ever since I knew ye, ye were so stubborn. That was a thing about you, never mind me. Then yer intuition, dont forget that!

Ye dont want me to dwell on the things that happen, she said, ye dont like it, ye never liked it. She was smiling round at me and her foot was near the cup on the carpet.

Honestly hen I dont know what ye mean.

Ye dont want me to dwell on it.

Well if it's the past ye're talking about I've seen what it does to people. It affects them. It gets them all twisted inside their head. It makes them bitter and they end up with sour faces.

That's daft, sour faces.

It's no daft it's a fact, I've seen it manys a time. People get choked by it.

The truth never hurt.

Dwelling on it did. Dwelling too much on it.

Fancy that.

I dont know what ye're getting at me for. Honestly hen, I dont.

Sour faces.

But that's what happens.

You didnay want to be serious. Boys.

I did but. I did want to be serious; that's one thing; so it irks me when ye say that hen, I didnay want to be serious, because I did, it wasnay me.

What do folk know. They think about a lot of things. Well at least they know a lot. If they didnt then they never would

229

and they would live to regret it. If they firmly believe it they accept it. And so it's unfair even to think it, if they tried harder, instead of blaming themself all the time, it's just a waste and it ends up sucking the life out ye, it's best making excuses so it isnay anybody to blame.

Hen there isnay anybody to blame, there's naybody to blame, it's only how it happened and it was a long time ago. It was, it's just raking it up and it's for nothing.

I dont like her name.

Joan.

I dont like it.

It was only her name, it was the lassie's name.

I dont like it. If I thought it was mainly to do with strength but I dont. And then when you're close to me yer face looks big. When I was a girl it was to do with strength, that was what it was. But now it goes funny and I have to listen hard. I'm talking but my voice is disappearing.

Of course it's no, of course it's no.

I have to listen hard, I do.

I let go her hand now and got up and walked about. I went through to give the kitchen a wee tidy. When I came back I thought she might be dozing. She was awake and she heard me. She still had her feet on that damn pouffe. I felt like flinging the thing out. It was our son bought it. She was straining forward trying to hear the telly; I turned it up a bit. She didnay use the remote, she didnay try; she would have got the hang of it easy. She was as stubborn as ever she was and she just gave me that look if I said something. I didnay like seeing these frown lines on her forehead and her skin because it was like it was always dry and I thought it was gony develop into an acne or a rash, it would break out in some way, it went red. I thought she was needing a vitamin. I telt the doctor and he says no to worry.

Then I was trying to get her to take the cod-liver oils but if I didnay remember she didnay. And she knew. I saw her smiling. Then if I wasnay there and I came in sudden she knew it. She did. She looked at me and she knew I was coming. It was a special thing about her, she always had that. Women's intuition. We had a good laugh about it. One time we were gon a sail down the water and she says no to bother booking because it would be too stormy and gales and everything and it would be cancelled, they wouldnay be able to bring the boat into the pier, and that was true, it turned out right enough. It was strong about her and manys the time she telt me things I had to mind when the kids were wee and then when they were aulder I had to go and get them if they were out at the dancing or something and she got an intuition there. I went along with it. I wouldnay take the chance no to. The kids got fed up but they had to put up with it and they knew my car would be there waiting across the road and I just used to say to the boy, Dont worry about it son if ye get a lumber, I'll gie her a drive up the road. Then the lassie, when she got aulder, I done the same. I dont care if ye're embarrassed, ye dont ignore yer intuition, when yer mother gets it ye listen, it's at yer peril.

It was these awkward positions she was always getting into, that damn pouffe and the pillow gon to one side so her back acted up even worse and there was nay need for it at all, it was bad enough as it was, ye could see it just by looking. I wouldnay have coped with it myself. I wish ye wouldnay put yer feet on that damn pouffe, I said, ye'll just suffer for it.

Constellation

When I got off the bus there was this star shining. It was hardly even dark yet there it was shining away. I could make out the five points like how ye drew it as a kid. Seeing it ye knew how the prehistorics picked them out and gave them names. That was the way I felt looking at it right at that very moment, except I wouldnay have known which name to give it.

But it was like this was a special night. The moonlight through the trees. Now the cloud shifting fast. Imagine taking a taxi and missing it all. That was what happened to these people with money, they were too busy rushing here and there. It was them got left behind. They never saw the space, they never got the time. My auld man was right. Money was supposed to buy ye everything but naw it didnay. It was the lack, not having it. The poor inherit the earth. That is what the bible tells ye. Wrong, says my da, it's theirs already.

I breathed the dampness from the leaves and the grass. The smell of river was in the air. What a night! People took alcohol, got stoned, shot junk into their veins. For what? For more than this? More than what I was experiencing right at that very moment? What would it matter if I didnt see her? What would it matter if I never saw her again in my whole life? Plus if every single friend she ever had, if every one was a lover? What would it matter?

I stopped walking and bowed my head, I was smiling at a certain thought, it always made me smile. I glanced up and for a moment my face was straight but then I chuckled and shook my head. I carried on walking. But it was definitely funny how it happened. How it crept up. Not like a bolt from the blue. That is one thing it wasnt because it was gradual, a really gradual thing; and when it arrived it was all-embracing.

I patted the side of my head, rubbing the hair. I had got a new haircut this morning and it was an amazing difference – really short. I was sick having to wash it and brush it all the time. Now it was a case of splashing it with water and drying it off with the towel, it straightened itself out.

But I liked this walk, it was different to where I lived, ye could smell the grass and the trees never mind see them. At that very minute she would be sitting in the bedroom, maybe with her sister. She wouldnay be in the living room with her parents. She didnay like sitting with them. And she never watched telly anyway, that was another thing about her, she liked being on her own, playing her music, looking through her auld papers, photographs and stuff, letters. Even her music was different, usually women singing. She had opera. She just sat there listening; sometimes with her eyes closed; it made her shiver; that was what she telt me.

Even being late I was dragging my feet. When I realised I was doing it I wondered how come. But sometimes I liked walking slow, no for any reason, it just gave ye a chance to think about things. The same gon to bed, I looked forward to it because I got the space for my head, I could just lie there, let my mind go. I liked to think about what she was doing, if she was sleeping, seeing her face on the pillow and touching it, touching her cheek. Sometimes I went early because I needed to think about her. I had to get her straight in my mind, check out things. I would try to see her in different situations and wonder how she was in them. I just couldnay picture it. Meeting auld people for instance, relatives, I couldnay imagine how she would be with them. I tried to picture her having a conversation and I couldnay. Even with the likes of her grannie and grandpa, I knew she saw them quite a lot but I couldnay imagine how it would be; her sitting there with them and talking, it was like frae another world. I didnay like wanking to her either. I did it but there was something no right about it.

I had seen maist of her body already. She changed her clothes in front of me. It was up to me what I done, if I looked away. I did look away but I did it like it was just a sort of fluke. There was a mirror there on the dressing table and sometimes ye couldnay help seeing, just depending how ye were sitting, ye saw her back sloping down and the top of her pants, her bra-strap pulled tight across her back, then her spine, it was a hollow, I thought she was too thin but I hadnay telt her.

The thing was and there was nay doubt about it, women were different. Even the way they spoke was different. The way they laughed. I noticed that with my sisters. What was it about the way they laughed? Cause they didnay have an adam's apple, maybe that was how. But one thing important was how they had friends. Men couldnay have friends the way women did. Women could have friends that were men but men couldnay have friends that were women. Maybe we could but we didnay. No eftir we left school. No even in school. Except maybe primary. No even then. Maybe before we went to school.

Ahead was the cluster of trees and bushes. The Wood. That was what the people round here called it. I felt spots of rain. But it was good. Refreshing. I couldnay see the sky anymore, just grey clouds. There was somebody coming, an auld person, a woman. There was naybody else in the vicinity except us two and ye wondered how come she was here, an auld woman, usually they're too scared to come out eftir dark, yet here she was, and she didnay seem to care at all. She was looking up at the sky. Probably wondering if she should stick up the brolly, maybe shelter beneath a tree if the rain got too heavy.

I would frighten her now if I approached too slow. I began whistling then walking ordinary so she wouldnay be scared. And she wasnt, she didnay look at me, I wasnay a threat. It was good that. I thought about the trees full of silent birds, some of them peering down at me. Waiting for the dawn. I didnay need the dawn, no to whistle.

Through at the end of the trees the streetlights caused a halo effect and the rain was amazing how it was visible, the separate drops, ye could see them cause of the bright glow. Separate drops of water. Rushing into the foliage. Refreshing the earth. But even as I watched it was slowing down. Then it went off altogether, it just stopped. When I reached the street I saw all the wee puddles, and the cracks in the pavement reflected the light. The moon was visible. I ran my hand along the roof of a parked car, skiting the water aff. Up by the corner at the next junction an icecream van stopped. A woman came out with a raincoat over her head. But she was wearing slippers! They flapped! She must have forgot! Now a boy ran from a close carrying a stack of empty ginger bottles. Memories memories. Myself in the same situation, how one of them had slipped out from under my arm and smashed, I was about twelve or something. What a disaster!

The things that go to make up yer life, where ye are, who ye are; all that. These bits and pieces. Millions of them, taking ye from childhood right the way up, so ye dont even notice, never catching the moment, ye can never catch it and hold onto it, not when the voice broke, the first sex, the lot; it was just something else; forever gone now; a total mystery:

even at the time. The boy is father of the man. Another of my auld man's. He was aye coming out with something. He was a funny auld guy in some ways.

Rain rain oh rain! Hail o rain, hail to thee!

I loved this place where she lived. I adored it. This place had my entire veneration. There was the window with the yellow and brown curtains.

This close, this close

What would I do if she was out? She might be out. Maybe she had gone out, me being late. She was never late for me. Just sometimes she couldnt meet me well then of course she wouldnt meet me, because she couldnt, because she was going elsewhere. But she was never late. I did it to her. I liked doing it. Crazy! But she never done it to me. I had her total trust so it didnay matter. She didnt feel the need. She said it to me: she trusted me, she didnt have to prove a single thing. Whatever it might be. Something or other. Who knows. Just I felt it myself occasionally, just now and again; to take it all in, breathe it in deep and just bloody enjoy it, the feeling, it was totally exhilarating. One night I followed her. She was meeting a guy. She telt me about him. He was just a friend. It was because things were getting to me and I just wanted to make sure. That was how I went. I didnay feel guilty about it. Ye were entitled to check up on somebody if ye were gieing them yer life and that was what I was doing, I was making that decision.

Nothing happened anyway. She just met him and they went into a lounge-bar up the town. I waited and then went hame. It was enough for me to see them the gether. The next night I saw her she telt me all about it. She was amazing and I think she was unique. At times I felt funny, I couldnay stop myself. I kept needing to think, I wanted space so I could work things out. When I was with her I couldnay. She was

236

too overpowering. It was like she filled every molecule, every point in the atmosphere, her presence, when I was with her, sometimes even when I wasnay, just thinking about her. Then another night there was a guy across the street, standing in the close opposite hers – not directly opposite, a few yards along – he was just standing there, this aulder guy; he was a man; at least forty by the looks of it. He hadnt noticed me, he was just staring across and it appeared to be her close he was staring at. I circled over about fifty yards on and doubled back on the same side pavement as him. Her bedroom light was on. That was where he was staring, it was obvious. A fucking peeping tom bastard, that was what I thought. I felt like going up and saying it to him. I got nearer, trying no to make it too obvious. He wasnay a big guy. I could have gave him a couple of inches. Then I thought maybe he was just waiting for somebody. Maybe he had locked himself out the house. It could have been anything. He looked totally normal. When I got up the stairs and rang the doorbell she answered herself. I waited till she led me ben the room and shut the door. I telt her to draw the curtains. There's a man standing in the close across the street, I said, I think he's looking up. She took a couple of seconds to take it in. Then what she did, she walked to the window and peered out, and she went: Mmm. That was all she did. She knew him, he stayed in the next street. He had a pal lived up the close. What is his pal no in? I said. I dont know, she said.

I remember we went out for a walk after that, and I had a wee bottle of martini and didnay tell her and when we went back to her room she gave this amazing smile when I took it out my pocket. Abracadabra.

Her eyes were huge. It was amazing how they were so huge. I aye wanted to hold her. Then how her breasts were under her top, they werenay big, just the right size. But her nipples were always noticeable, ye always saw them poking out. At the same time I thought she was too thin. No her bum. The right proportions. She wore jeans with a fancy design she made herself, she knitted it on, it was her own pattern. That was typical. That was exactly the kind of thing she did. It was like all the rest of the stuff in her room. All the different things she had; keepsakes and crazy stuff, all kinds of stuff, photographs and crazy pictures cut out from magazines and books.

Now here I was tonight. She took me in as usual and I started telling her about the work-placement I was having to take. I had had an idea about the two of us getting some cash saved and going away for a holiday. I was thinking about doing a bit of hitching, maybe France or something or else Holland or Denmark, maybe Belgium. There was a bus ye could get from London straight to Paris. We could do it on the cheap, hitch it down from Glasgow. My uncle done it when he was my age. He went to France. There was a place there took ye on for grape picking. It depends on the time of year. He still had the address and thought the farmer guy would still be in business, if he was he would take me on nay bother. The wages werenay great but if ye had a tent he gave ye a field to camp in. There was water and all the facilities. It would be great. I watched her pick a cassette and stick it into the machine. The music started. D'ye fancy going for a walk? I said.

No yet.

Maybe later?

She gave me a funny look and then said, I've a friend staying a couple of nights, his name's Ohgoost, spelled like August, he's from Holland, I met him in a pizza-place up the town, he's a student. He was here to see Scotland but it was raining all the time and then the midges done him

roundabout Loch Lomond. Somebody stole his wallet, they took it out his rucksack. He's stranded.

D'ye mean he's here in the house?

He's having a bath. It's the first he's had for four days. He should be out any minute. She came close to me and touched my head, she drew her hand up the back of it, making the bristles go up. You've had a haircut, she said, it's nice. D'ye want a coffee?

I couldnay move, I just stood there, the feeling of her doing it.

Away she went. I was looking about her room, it was so wee. I sat down on the edge of the bed. There was nothing she did surprised me. Except when it happened, when it happened it did.

I dont know what I thought. There was nay signs of the guy. She took him home because he was stranded with nowhere to go. What else should she have done?

Then his rucksack. It was a funny place to carry a wallet. Then go leaving it about for all-comers. That was one thing could stick in yer mind. Surely ye knew, surely people knew? It was a thing ye learned. Ye learned it in Glasgow anyway.

Ye always have these visions of Holland people, they look like moviestars, famous tennisplayers or something, they're all beautiful.

Who else would have brought him home? Who else would have even got talking to the guy? How did she even know he was stranded? Did he come up and tell her, did she just guess? Was it him started the conversation? There was this absentminded way she could be. I could imagine her seeing him and knowing something was up, and just asking him what it was, what the trouble was, I could actually imagine her doing that; out the blue, him being surprised; I could imagine it. It was the kind of thing she did. This thing about

239

friends. That was what she called them: friends. I never knew what that meant: friends. No when she said it. She even made it sound different. It wasnay anything to do with it being sexy. I had thought about that, if that was what was funny about it. But it wasnay. It was like something else, a touch of magic. Ye saw something for the first time. Or thought ye did. One thing I knew was I had never ever had a friend, no in the sense she was talking about, except maybe her. When she said 'friends' it included everything. A friend for her was somebody ye gave yerself tae completely. I dont mean sex. Even if it was an auld dosser on the street. Once she said that to me and I made a joke about what do ye do, d'ye go up and fling yer arms round him? How no? she said. If it's a friend then ye'd do anything. You and me are friends. Whatever you want I'll do.

Whatever you want I'll do. It made ye shiver when she spoke like that because ye knew she meant it. Every word. Her eyes staring straight at ye till ye had to look away. Or else say something. Change the subject; ye knew ye were gony get a hardon and ye wouldnay be able to stop it if ye did. And ye knew she knew. And she felt sorry for ye! It was terrible but at the same time the best feeling imaginable.

This Holland guy would turn out like that. He would send her letters. She would send him letters. It would be like a movie.

Where things like that were concerned we seemed to be on different wavelengths. I got my sisters talking about it one night, they telt me they could have men for friends. But the way they said it it wasnay the same as her. I couldnay put my finger on what it was.

But usually always when she said something it left me silent, no having anything to say. I couldnay challenge her, even if I wanted to. I wasny even sure she knew herself. Once I did try telling her about some of these guys she saw: she maybe

thought they were friends but that might no be the way the guys themselves would see it, they might just have been eftir her. But she wasnay naive. Naive was the last thing. She was just about the sharpest most intelligent person I ever knew. It was me that was naive. I was waiting there for the coffee, staring out the window. There was a chap on the door and in came the Holland guy.

He was nay different to what I had thought; tall and blond and blue eyes. Looking fresh from the bath, his hair all damp and streaky. Then the jeans and shirt; he must have been loaded, his family must have been. And I wouldnay have called him friendly, no at first sight. He spoke good English, better than me by a long margin. Hello, he said, you are Peter? He moved to shake hands with me. Where is Annie?

She's making coffee.

Yes. He smiled. She is a good woman. She is going to college soon.

To college?

She is going soon?

I dont know.

Ah. He smiled, looking about her room. He pointed at the cassette. I like this song, very much.

It's good, I said, yeh.

She came in with a tray and the cups of coffee, a packet of biscuits. Are ye sure ye dont want anything to eat? she said to him.

No no.

Her maw and da were letting him sleep on the sofa. If they hadnay agreed to that he would have slept in her room. That was what like she was. But I was beginning to relax, now I saw them the gether, I knew it was okay. This strange guy sitting in her room, handsome guy with money, a foreigner, it was just how I knew it would be. I felt strong. I wasnay worried about him, although he was big, it didnay matter, no in the physical way, like if it was a fight, I think I could have battered him, I would have waded in. But it wasnay that, nothing like it. It was as if she was mine, before she would ever be his. I saw her as just young and I thought God she's got to get protected, anything could happen to her. And it was something between me and him, the Holland guy. He knew. We baith knew. I watched him, the ways he spoke to her and looked at her. Obviously she was sexy, there was nothing could be done about that, when ye looked at her, ye had to see her.

She was the most beautiful sexiest woman I ever saw. But she was too open to getting hurt. Except the likes of me and the Holland guy, for the likes of us it was taboo. He might have wanted to touch her but he wouldnay have been able to. I felt like that myself. I was always wanting to touch her. She let me. When I did she just used to watch me like she was wondering what I was gony do next.

Now the guy started talking about things. He didnay talk about himself but, it was things he had seen. She was all agog. She loved hearing about stuff. The college thing came up. She smiled across at me.

The Good Times

How feeble my defences were. The bed was damp with sweat and my eyes were right onto the strange shadows on the wall, coming through the strange curtains my wife bought not too long ago. Even beyond the act of waking up my mind had gone to the most ambiguous things in the entire fucking room. Yet another dream to do with nonatheist concepts like devils and other supernatural beings. The only consolation is that within the dream itself I had taken on the role of head man – not head man, it was just I was having to do some damn action in the face of these horrible fucking things that were befalling us all. And I was having to head northeast, up farther than Aberdeen. Oh jesus land of my forefathers for the past millennium. Then calling this person on the phone for some sort of advice, or to do with some vaguely businesslike, vaguely down-to-earth chat, only to discover that he was overcome with terror during the phonecall. At that point I fought myself out of sleep (so-called).

Yet the moonlight through these strange curtains making these strange patterns on the wall.

The whole fucking house is strange, that was my one act of reason. Maybe it was only death, a wee warning, a subconscious method of diverting the crazy side of my imagination; only death. My lungs were caving in. The best of my flesh was dissipating into a vapour and this vapour was leaving my pores and soaking the sheets, and these sheets were a nylon kind of shit so the vapour became liquid and clung to me, sodden and thickly damp like sperm or something, jesus

243

christ. And my belly felt like the size of a house, full of wind and fuck knows what, the effects of a king prawn satay too late in the evening; worse than cheese, the effect it has on my system what with the medication, part of which is the dire absences: caffeine and alcohol.

I crept through the lobby, not loudly but not too surreptitiously either, turning on lights I thought were reasonably dim, but no sooner was I in the living-room (sweet phrase) than a presence appeared behind me, my wife in her nightdress wondering what was wrong?

Nothing.

The noise woke me.

Sorry, I didnay realise I was making any noise.

What is it?

Ach, bad dreams just.

She was thirsty. I was thirsty. But it hadnt got me to the stage of doing something about it. Yet here she was and had taken care of that consideration immediately, and was smiling as she got herself a glass of soft something or other – coke probably – and she smiled again, bidding me goodnight, returning to her sanctuary; it was alright for her, but unless she could take me with her into her dreams then here I was staying. I had smiled in reply to her, letting her think I had everything under control. Besides being the male I am older than her so there were all these protective roles I was aye having to adopt. What was going to happen to me. For the rest of my life. Which ebbed from me. Even as I sat there, it ebbed from me. I heard her creaking onto the bed, I switched on the television. Half naked lassies diving about to some incredible scene of crashing music and crashing lights. Why were teenagers like that! If they only knew what I knew, if only that, poor wee bastards, their innocence. I looked for resemblances, trying to find the boy who looked like me, the girl who looked like one of my early loves, the girl with the look of a woman. The girls I loved were always women, they acted like women and they made me feel like they were women. I looked for girls like that, I looked for normality. But there was no normality. The boys seemed like men with bad manners and violent ways, and the girls seemed vulnerable, vulnerable, oh so bloody fucking vulnerable, vulnerable. The girls relied on these boys, relied on them to be boys. But they had come too quickly to adulthood, they had been forced to recognise their own limitations, they werent going to play for Rangers, they werent going to play for anybody; and they werent getting the good job, they werent getting this that or anything. Fucking fuck all man nothing, they were on the scrapheap. Even the mild boys, the ones who liked the girls and enjoyed seeing them lark around, they were timid, they were acting up to the rough tough bastards, letting them take control, letting their values dominate the proceedings.

Oh christ, I needed caffeine. I needed black coffee but was allowing myself tea, only tea, not even strong tea, some sort of peppermint shite.

But the nightmares could have gone for this night. Now the tricky part began. I switched the television off, thinking of the teenagers being blanked back into their own privacy, away from my prying eyes. Adults prey on young people, in many many ways. Their life-force. I could see them shaking in trepidation, moving through time so slowly they can cry out for help on the road but as in slow motion the help – if it comes – is distorted, it isnt help, it's disguised, so much so it has been transformed into yet another obstacle. But these teenagers, I felt like they had saved my life, my sanity perhaps.

Then there were all these possessions. Most of what I owned was useless. I'm talking about my stuff, my personal stuff. It was a load of junk; I didnt keep these things for any

245

purpose, the only motive was the wishes of others, it was they who expressed to me the wish that I treasure something and so I treasured somethings, stuff, fuck knows what, it meant nothing to me, stereotypical fatherly possessions, an ancient deerstalker hat my youngest boy got me out a jumble-sale, a strange-looking toy bicycle, a cigar I wasnay gony smoke but had got as a present, and so on.

The things that meant something to me I was *forced* to accept, to tolerate, to countenance as an effect of my years, in exchange for the gift of longevity, the gift of middle age: my physical ailments.

If the truth be told I was fond of my physical ailments. I was even fond of my nightmares, they were the stuff of life. It was life that forced me awake. How many times had this happened, this forcing myself out of sleep as an act of survival: to have continued enduring such sleep was to forsake life, it was to give up breathing, give up living, because I knew for certain, about these bad dreams and nightmares, that the true extension was death. It wasnt so much feebleness as tiredness, an exhaustion close to complete. These teenage males must have known this. When I was one I knew it for sure. I kept clear of old people, they made me face death and infirmity, they made me face a future of dwindling strengths. It was this the lassies could cope with, they did cope with, they coped with it so well. It was a crucial distinction between the sexes. I even recognised that this had existed between my own kids when they were that age; they had exhibited these very distinctions. Yeh.

This was a genuine insight. I still dreaded going to bed though, I dreaded it. I wondered if my wife was asleep again. Without a doubt it was the same for her; sometimes I could just lie there listening to her breathe, watching her eyelids twitch. But these are the good times.